WE SHALL OVERCOME

someday.
Oh, deep in
my heart,
I do believe
That we shall
overcome
someday.

COLORED

WE SHALL OVERCOME

THE HISTORY OF THE
AMERICAN CIVIL RIGHTS MOVEMENT

Reggie Finlayson

LERNER PUBLICATIONS COMPANY · MINNEAPOLIS

To the parents who lost children in the civil rights movement, and to those children, who made a way where there was none before.

My thanks to the choirs in black Baptist churches for their music; to Bernice Ragon of Sweet Honey in the Rock for insight into congregational singing; and to Chief Bey for his explanations of the rhythms of African dance. Thanks also to civil rights leaders in Milwaukee who talked with me, and to the patient editorial department of Lerner Publications Company.

Lerner Publications Company
A division of Lerner Publishing Group
241 First Avenue North
Minneapolis, MN 55401 U.S.A.

Website address: www.lernerbooks.com

Library of Congress Cataloging-in-Publication Data

Finlayson, Reggie.
    We shall overcome : the history of the American civil rights movement / by Reggie Finlayson.
        p.   cm. — (People's history)
        Summary: Uses the words of spirituals and other music of the time to frame a discussion of the civil rights movement in the United States, focusing on specific people, incidents, and court cases.
        Includes bibliographical references and index.
        ISBN: 0–8225–0647–5 (lib. bdg. : alk. paper)
        1. African Americans—Civil rights—History—20th century—Juvenile literature. 2. Civil rights movements—United States—History—20th century—Juvenile literature. 3. United States—Race relations—Juvenile literature. [1. African Americans—Civil rights—History—20th century. 2. Civil rights movements—History—20th century. 3. Race relations.] I. Title. II. Series.
        E185.61 .F48 2003
        323.1'196073'009045   2002000954

Manufactured in the United States of America
1 2 3 4 5 6 – JR – 08 07 06 05 04 03

Contents

A NOTE TO READERS

In trying to faithfully construct a portrait of the civil rights movement in the United States in the 1950s and 1960s, I struggled with the question of language about race. Over the years, African Americans have worn many labels, including "colored," "Negro," "black," "Afro-American," and "African descended." All these terms are weighted with historical and political meaning.

As this book is being published, "African American" is the term most often used to describe the people who launched the civil rights movement in the United States. I used this term sometimes in writing this book. But I found it awkward to describe whites in a similar way. Calling whites "Euro-Americans" seemed forced.

Americans in the 1950s and 1960s looked at things differently than Americans in the twenty-first century. At that time, African Americans were not seen mostly in terms of their origins in Africa. They were identified by their color.

By the end of the 1960s, the term "black" had replaced "Negro" and "colored." In this book, I have used the labels "black" and "white" often. These words are simple and balanced. They also express the gulf that so deeply divided the races in this era.

— *Reggie Finlayson*

WE SHALL OVERCOME

We shall overcome.
We shall overcome.
We shall overcome someday.
Oh, deep in my heart,
I do believe
That we shall overcome someday.
　　　　—song of the American
　　　　　civil rights movement

Fog engulfed the Smoky Mountains that Saturday night in April 1960 when county deputies raided the Highlander Folk School in the small mountain town of Monteagle, Tennessee. Like the big cats that had once prowled the region, the men moved in under cover of night. Slivers of light sliced the dark beneath the school's windows. Then one of the men found the power junction and cut the electricity, killing the lights.

Inside, nearly one hundred students from nineteen states had gathered to discuss ways to end segregation (the forced separation of blacks and whites). These students and thousands of others like them all around the United States were a powerful force in the civil rights movement that was actively protesting segregation and other injustices.

Led by a Tennessee lawyer, Abe Sloan, the deputies entered the school carrying flashlights that illuminated their guns and billy clubs at the ready. Striding back and forth among the student activists, the men accused teacher Septima Clark of illegally selling beer. They were shutting down the school.

Highlander had long challenged Tennessee's segregation laws and had suffered earlier raids. So the staff recognized the type of men they called "deputized thugs." Many students had had firsthand experience with groups such as the Ku Klux Klan (KKK), which used terrorist tactics to keep blacks "in their place." No one knew what would happen this night, but many students feared they might be killed.

Jamila Jones, just sixteen, later said she felt her own fear and that of others. Trying not to panic, she began humming a tune she had just learned. Then the words slipped out: "We shall overcome. / We shall overcome. / We shall overcome someday. / Oh, deep in my heart, / I do believe / That we shall overcome someday." One by one, the other students joined her.

Opposite, *this young woman was jailed for her role in the American civil rights movement in the 1960s.* **Above,** *members of the Ku Klux Klan, a racist terrorist group formed in the 1800s.*

"There seemed to be a need to say to the men, 'We are not afraid,'" Jones remembered. She began leading the group in some new words: "We are not afraid, /We are not afraid, /We are not afraid today." Soon the new lyrics were ringing through the school. One deputy snapped, "If you have to sing, do you have to sing so loud?"

Amazingly, the deputies seemed unnerved and began to back down. "It was just like nature came into that room," Jones said. "They retreated very nervously and had to leave."

In the court case that followed concerning the charge of selling beer, the state presented no evidence of liquor being sold. (In fact, Septima Clark never drank liquor.) Even so, the state won. It confiscated the school's lands. Highlander's founder, Myles Horton, then reestablished the school in Knoxville, Tennessee.

Despite this setback, the students never forgot the victory of that dark night. They returned to their communities with the story of how they had faced down the deputies with nothing more than their own dignity and courage. And they taught the song they had learned—including Jamila Jones's new verse—to people back home, encouraging them to fight for the rights white Americans enjoyed. The song seemed to hold a great promise. Nothing could stop the ultimate success of this movement.

PAID BY THE SWORD

A long, grim history preceded the assault on Highlander Folk School. African Americans first arrived in the English colonies in North America as slaves in 1619. Many years later, "We Shall Overcome" was sung by slaves in southern plantation fields. Working endless hours, and sometimes whipped and beaten, slaves prayed for strength to make it through a day. Not surprisingly, the earliest lyrics of "We Shall Overcome" focused on survival and faith: "Oh Jesus, take my hand, /I do believe, /I'll be alright someday."

The Emancipation Proclamation, issued by President Abraham Lincoln during the Civil War (1861–1865), freed slaves in the South.

"We pray that this scourge of war may speedily pass away," Lincoln told the nation. But, he warned, the North would not stop fighting for the Union cause and for abolition (freedom for slaves) until "every drop of blood drawn with the lash shall be paid by another drawn with the sword." Hundreds of thousands of soldiers, black and white, died in the fighting.

After the war, the Thirteenth Amendment to the U.S. Constitution abolished slavery. The Fourteenth Amendment protected freed slaves. And the Fifteenth Amendment gave black men the right to vote. Blacks flocked to two new colleges for African Americans (Howard University in Washington, D.C., and Fisk University in Nashville, Tennessee). Thousands of African Americans registered to vote. The Civil Rights Act of 1875 granted blacks equal access to public accommodations and forbade job discrimination.

All these new laws, however, could not create new attitudes. When asked by Congress to report on racial attitudes, one man declared that most whites were "unable to conceive of the Negro as having any rights at all."

JIM CROW

Viewing African Americans as inferior led to a system known as Jim Crow. Jim Crow was the name of a minstrel show character created by performer Thomas "Daddy" Rice. To play the part of Jim Crow, the white actor wore blackface (makeup that mocks the appearance of black skin) and mimicked an elderly black man. Jim Crow was so popular that white audiences soon linked the name to any black man. Gradually the name came to apply to all the laws and customs that kept blacks and whites separated in society. Many states began to create "black codes"—laws limiting the gains of the Civil Rights Act.

By the late 1800s, Jim Crow seemed to govern every detail of daily life, especially in the South. African Americans were expected to use a title of respect when addressing any white. They had to step off the sidewalk when encountering whites. They had to drink at water fountains marked "colored." African Americans could certainly not be intimate with white people.

Laws segregating blacks forced them into separate seating on buses and trains, separate schools, and even separate neighborhoods. Some states made blacks take impossibly difficult tests before letting them register to vote. (One man flunked a voter registration test after being asked how many bubbles were in a bar of soap.) All-white primaries kept black candidates from running for office.

In 1896 the U.S. Supreme Court heard a case called *Plessy v. Ferguson.* Homer Plessy, a black man, sued a railroad company with segregated seating. His side argued that the Fourteenth Amendment made segregation illegal. But the Court ruled that separate accommodations for blacks and whites were legal as long as they were equal.

Beginning in the late 1800s, Jim Crow laws and customs segregated almost every detail of daily life in some regions of the United States, particularly in the South.

"Separate but equal" became the official doctrine of the South. Under Jim Crow, however, separate was hardly ever equal. On trains, blacks found themselves crowded onto fewer and shabbier cars. Their separate schools and hospitals were ill equipped and run-down.

Jim Crow customs were enforced by vigilantes who sometimes beat violators or burned their homes and businesses. Lynching (murder by an angry mob) was not uncommon. According to journalist Ida B. Wells, more than ten thousand African Americans were lynched between 1878 and 1898. One violent incident occurred on Sunday afternoon, April 23, 1899, outside Newton, Georgia. Sam Hose, a black man, had gotten into a fight with his white employer, Alfred Cranford. Some witnesses later said Hose struck Cranford, killing him, after Cranford pulled a gun. A mob of about two thousand whites then gathered and burned Hose to death.

Thousands of African Americans were lynched in the United States from the late 1800s to the mid-1900s.

LIFE GOES ON

Despite such horrors, African Americans built schools, homes, and businesses. They made churches the center of community life. Songs of hope lived on. In 1901 a Methodist minister from Philadelphia, Pennsylvania, penned some new lyrics to a familiar tune: "I will overcome, / I will overcome, / I will overcome, someday. / Oh, down in my heart, / I do believe, / I will overcome someday."

In the following decades, blacks founded several civil rights organizations. The National Association for the Advancement of Colored People (NAACP), founded in 1909, aimed to end racial violence, stop job discrimination, and promote equal laws.

After the United States entered World War II in 1941, U.S. industry began producing the tools of war. To demand a fair share of war-related jobs, black union leader Asa Philip Randolph proposed that blacks march on Washington, D.C. President Franklin D. Roosevelt didn't want a massive protest in the nation's capital at a time when the United States was trying to lead the world in a fight for justice and democracy. Randolph and other organizers agreed to cancel the march when Roosevelt agreed to ban job discrimination in federal government and in war industries.

Songs of resistance such as "We Shall Overcome" still had meaning. In the mid-1940s, South Carolina tobacco workers adapted the song when they went on strike for better working conditions. They sang: "We will win our pay. / Oh, deep in my heart, / I do believe, / That we will overcome someday."

World War II ended in 1945 and American troops—including more than one million African Americans—came home to ticker tape parades. Most white veterans hoped to recreate the lives they'd left behind. African American veterans, on the other hand, hoped for a better life than a life under Jim Crow. President Harry Truman recognized the service of African Americans by desegregating the armed services in 1948.

The fight against Jim Crow finally connected with the song "We Shall Overcome" in the civil rights movement that began in the 1950s.

At stake were equal education, equal housing, equal voting rights, equal access to public accommodations, and equal treatment in the workplace and financial world. The movement sparked a revolution in race relations. Unlike other revolutions, however, this one used peaceful methods.

Martin Luther King Jr. became a symbol of this movement. But tens of thousands of nameless people earned its success. Black and white, rich and poor, worked together for change. Sometimes they faced angry mobs. Some of them were killed. Their struggle took nearly two decades and terrific courage. This is the story of how, in the end, the American civil rights movement of the 1950s and 1960s did overcome, and how its progress was chronicled in its poetry and song.

***Thousands of ordinary Americans joined Martin Luther King Jr.*
(speaking into microphone)** *in the American civil rights movement.*

THIS LITTLE LIGHT

This little light of mine,
I'm gonna let it shine.
This little light of mine,
I'm gonna let it shine,
Let it shine,
Let it shine,
Let it shine.

—song of the American
civil rights movement

In the early 1950s, blacks and whites were kept separate, especially in the South. Seventeen states had laws requiring separate but equal schools for blacks and whites. Almost always, separate schools meant unequal schools. The schools of Clarendon County, South Carolina, were typical. They had nearly three times as many black students as whites in 1950. The school board spent $179 per year on each white student, compared to $43 for each black student. The schools for black students were little more than shacks. Teachers were woefully underpaid.

Consequently, at the urging of the NAACP, twenty parents signed a petition suing the school district. Harry and Liza Briggs were the first to sign. But at the hotel where Liza worked, the owner quickly pressured her to remove her name. "The White Council of Summerton came down and told [my boss] if he didn't fire the women who signed the petition that they would close the business down," said Briggs. Briggs refused to back down, even though white citizens councils (groups formed to protect the advantages of white business owners) had the influence to get black workers fired and to blacklist them from jobs. "I didn't want to [remove my name] because we would be hurting the children," Liza Briggs explained. "I'd rather give up my job and keep my name on there." Within two weeks, she was unemployed.

Many others connected to the suit faced similar consequences. People were fired. Banks called in loans or refused to issue new ones. Stores refused to sell black farmers seeds for planting or tools for harvesting.

When the case was heard in a federal district court, it failed. The court recognized the unequal educational opportunity. Still, it simply ordered black students to wait until improvements could be made to their segregated schools.

PRINCE EDWARD COUNTY

Even before the Briggs case was filed in Clarendon County, Robert R. Moton High School in Prince Edward County, Virginia, was overflowing. The state had offered a grant for an addition in 1947, but the school board had refused the matching funds. Many seats sat vacant in a nearby high school for whites. Instead of transferring black students, however, the school board scheduled classes in the Robert R. Moton auditorium, in a bus, and in three flimsy, temporary buildings that the students dubbed "the tar paper shacks." Meanwhile, the board spent three times more on white students than on blacks.

In April 1951, sixteen-year-old Barbara Rose Johns decided to demand a new school. Johns and nine others tricked the principal into leaving the building, then faked an announcement calling all classes to the auditorium. Organizers escorted teachers out of the school as Johns called for a strike. Everyone joined her when she marched out.

Even though the superintendent threatened to expel the students, they stayed out of school for the next three days. Then the students, their parents, and other supporters gathered to hear lawyers from the

NAACP speak. When the lawyers warned that students could be expelled or even jailed for striking, the students shouted that the jails could not hold all of them. Given this support, the NAACP decided to sue Prince Edward County—not for a better school building, but for desegregated schools.

The students continued striking through the end of the school year. Even so, the NAACP lost its case. The court ruled that segregation was based on custom, not law. It could not be legally regulated.

BROWN V. BOARD OF EDUCATION

The lawsuits in Clarendon and Prince Edward Counties were just two of several cases the NAACP took on. Another similar lawsuit had been tried and lost in Wilmington, Delaware. Still another came from the District of Columbia. The head of the Legal Defense Fund of the NAACP, Thurgood Marshall, wanted to take all these cases to the U.S. Supreme Court. He decided to argue them as a group. Then he added one more case—a situation involving Linda Brown of Topeka, Kansas.

Linda was a seven-year-old who took a bus to an all-black elementary school each day. There was an elementary school just a few blocks from her home, but it was reserved for white students. To catch the bus, Linda had to walk through a railroad yard and through several busy intersections. Telling the story years later, she remembered walking stiffly in the cold, tears freezing on her cheeks. The situation angered Linda's parents, Oliver and Leola Brown.

The local NAACP gathered together thirteen parents in Topeka and asked them to take their children to the nearest school on the first day of classes. Once the parents were denied permission to enroll their children, the NAACP could proceed with a class action lawsuit. Linda Brown later remembered her father as "a mild man" who took "his plump seven-year-old daughter by the hand and walked to the all-white school and tried without success to enroll his daughter." When this case came before a federal district court, the judges ruled in favor of the school board.

The injustice of segregated schools was one of the first issues tackled by civil rights activists of the 1950s.

Eventually the U.S. Supreme Court agreed to Thurgood Marshall's request for an appeal. The Court heard the cases from Kansas, South Carolina, Virginia, Delaware, and the District of Columbia together under the name *Brown v. Board of Education of Topeka, Shawnee County, Kansas.*

Marshall's strategy was to prove that separate was not equal. Wherever students were segregated, blacks were shortchanged. "I told the staff that we had to try this case just like any other in which you would try to prove damages to your client," said Marshall of preparations for the case. "If your car ran over my client, you'd have to pay up, and my function as an attorney would be to put experts on the stand to testify to how much damage was done. We needed exactly that kind of evidence in the school cases." But how could anyone prove that the system of separate schools was hurting some children?

To prove damage, the NAACP legal team asked a psychologist, Kenneth Clark, to conduct psychological tests on the black students involved. Clark and his wife, Mamie Phipps, had done similar tests a decade earlier. Clark began interviewing sixteen black students in Clarendon County ranging in age from six to nine. To test their attitudes, he showed them a white doll and a brown doll and questioned them about the dolls. He asked if one doll was "inferior." Most children said yes and pointed to the brown doll. The most disturbing moment for Clark came when he said, "Now show me the doll that's most like you." Many of the children got visibly upset as they identified themselves as being most like the "inferior" doll.

Clark went on to compare these students with others in integrated schools. His study showed that black students in segregated schools felt inferior to those in integrated schools. As he had written in the *Journal of Experimental Education* ten years earlier, "Segregation . . . is the way in which a society tells a group of human beings that they are inferior."

Thurgood Marshall (left) *hired psychologists to demonstrate that African American students were being harmed by segregated schools.*

The U.S. Supreme Court's ruling declared that Clark's testimony was key. On May 17, 1954, the Court handed down a unanimous decision that stated: "In the field of public education, the doctrine of 'separate but equal' has no place. Separate educational facilities are inherently unequal." With those words, the twenty-one states with segregated schools were ordered to integrate.

Southern segregationists dubbed the day of the *Brown* decision Black Monday (after Black Thursday, the day in 1929 that signaled an economic downturn called the Great Depression). A Mississippi senator, James Eastland, expressed their dismay. "On May 17, 1954," he declared, "the Constitution of the United States was destroyed." On the following day, an editorial in the *Jackson Daily News* announced, "Mississippi cannot and will not try to abide by such a decision."

EMMETT TILL

Instead of narrowing the gulf between whites and blacks, the *Brown* decision seemed to widen it. The intensity of the racial hatred surrounding the decision was evident outside the schools as well. A chilling example can be found in the story of Emmett Till.

According to accounts given later, it was about five o'clock on Wednesday evening, August 25, 1955, when Emmett Till and his cousin Curtis Jones stopped at Bryant's Meat and Grocery Market in Money, Mississippi. Fourteen-year-old Emmett, who lived in Chicago, Illinois, was in town visiting relatives.

At the store, the two boys began talking with some other boys about their romantic exploits. Emmett pulled a photograph of a white girl from his wallet and bragged that she was his girlfriend. Staring in disbelief, the local boys peppered the newcomer with questions. "Hey," one of them said. "There's a girl in that store there. I bet you won't go in there and talk to her."

The "girl" was Carolyn Bryant, a married woman with two children. She was white. The boys taunted Emmett, daring him to speak to Bryant, who owned the store with her husband.

Emmett was a big-city boy from the North. Probably he didn't know he should have shrugged off the dare. Instead he went into the store and bought some candy. Turning to leave, he said, "Bye, baby," to Carolyn Bryant.

Back at the cabin of their uncle, a sharecropper (farmer) named Mose Wright, the boys said nothing. But a local girl who heard about the incident was telling people, "When that lady's husband comes back there is going to be trouble." Ray Bryant, a trucker, was away but would be back soon.

Sometime after midnight three days later, Mose Wright heard a rap on his door. Ray Bryant and his brother-in-law, J. W. Milam, stood there in the dark. "Bring out the boy who done all the talkin'," Bryant ordered. Wright pleaded that his nephew was only fourteen and didn't know the ways of the South.

"How old are you, preacher?" they asked. Wright answered, "Sixty-four." "If you cause any trouble," they warned, "you'll never live to be sixty-five." Then they pushed Emmett into a car and drove off.

Emmett's cousin called the police and accused Bryant and Milam of kidnapping. Accounts vary about what happened next. Some witnesses reported seeing Emmett with a group of men that included Bryant and Milam.

At some point, Emmett Till died. His bloated body was found in the Tallahatchie River three days after he disappeared. He was naked and had a bullet in his head. His skull was crushed on one side. Barbed wire held a small mechanical fan to his neck. One of his eyes had been gouged out. When authorities arrested Bryant and Milam, they added the charge of murder to that of kidnapping.

When local people heard about Emmett's body, even the staunchest segregationists were shocked. Intent on putting the matter to rest as soon as possible, the sheriff's department planned a speedy burial in Mississippi. But Mamie Bradley, Emmett's mother, insisted the body be shipped back to her in Chicago. The sheriff honored her wish but directed that the casket remain closed.

Throngs of reporters joined Mamie Bradley when she met Emmett's casket at the train station in Chicago. Defiantly, she opened the casket immediately. "Lord take my soul," she gasped. Then she asked the reporters, "Have you ever sent a loved son on vacation and had him returned to you in a pine box, so horribly battered and water logged that someone needs to tell you this sickening sight is your son—lynched?"

Bradley had her son's body taken to Rainer Funeral Home. She postponed a funeral for four days and left Emmett's casket open for the thousands of visitors who paid their respects. She was determined, she said, to "let the world see what they did to my boy."

Emmett Till's mother, Mamie Bradley (**front center**) *at his funeral in September 1955*

Emmett Till. Emmett was just fourteen years old when he was lynched.

News of Emmett Till's murder swept through the nation like a chilly winter wind. The Negro Press Association and newspapers such as the *Chicago Defender, Pittsburgh Courier,* and *Baltimore Afro-American* reported the story to their mostly black audiences. Magazines such as *Jet, Ebony,* and *The Crisis* quickly followed with their own stories.

Meanwhile, Mose Wright was receiving anonymous threats warning him to leave Mississippi. He was definitely scared.

THE VERDICT

Two weeks after Emmett Till's funeral, Bryant and Milam went on trial for murder. Five of the top lawyers from the area agreed to represent them. Many whites rallied in support, raising ten thousand dollars for a defense fund. Newspaper editorials in the white press attacked civil rights advocates for calling the murder a lynching.

The state appointed a special prosecutor. No budget and no staff were allocated, however. Any hope of convicting Bryant and Milam lay with the witnesses, but any witness could expect to be threatened or harmed. Curtis Jones's mother forbade him to testify. "My mother was afraid something would happen to me like something happened to Emmett Till," Jones said.

Despite the threats against him, Mose Wright did testify. The court-room was packed the day he took the stand. Reporters and spectators turned out as if the trial were a presidential campaign stop. When the prosecutor asked Wright if the people who had kidnapped Emmett were in the courtroom, Wright pointed at the two defendants.

Other witnesses also came forward. Till's mother testified that the dead boy pulled from the Tallahatchie River was her son. Other witnesses had seen Emmett with Bryant and Milam or heard the sounds of Emmett being beaten.

The trial lasted just five days. On September 23, 1955, after thirty minutes of deliberation, the jury returned a verdict: not guilty. In a separate trial on the charge of kidnapping, Bryant and Milam were again found not guilty.

Bryant and Milam later admitted to killing the boy from Chicago. They had only meant to scare him, they said. But Emmett wouldn't express shame for acting too familiar with a white woman. "What else could we do?" Milam asked during a newspaper interview. "He was hopeless. I'm no bully; . . . I like niggers in their place. . . . But I just decided it was time a few people got put on notice."

Milam's notion of the right kind of lesson for an African American boy contrasted sharply with that of the U.S. Supreme Court in its *Brown* ruling. Bridging the enormous difference between the two would not be easy.

AIN'T GONNA RIDE

Ain't gonna ride them buses
*   no more,*
Ain't gonna ride no more.
Why don't all the white folk know
That I ain't gonna ride no more.
        —song of the American
            civil rights movement

In the winter of 1955 (more than a year after the *Brown* decision), Montgomery, Alabama, was still a Jim Crow town. All its public accommodations, including city buses, had been legally segregated since 1900. The local bus company hired only white drivers. And riders were separated by race. Whites sat in the front of the bus. African Americans sat in the back. To get there, they had to pay in front, get off the bus, and reenter through a rear door.

Between the section for whites and blacks was a kind of no-man's land. Seats in this section could be claimed by anyone. Even in this section, however, whites and blacks were not supposed to sit in the same row with one another. Sometimes a bus got overcrowded, and white riders couldn't find a seat. In that case, the law said blacks in the no-man's zone had to give up their seats—but only if they could find a free seat in the black section.

Since no clear line divided black and white seating, bus drivers policed the situation as they pleased. Some drivers made black riders give up their seats, even when no seats were available in the black section. It didn't matter that most of the riders were black.

"THIS CAN'T GO"

African Americans had long protested these discriminatory practices. Baseball great Jackie Robinson was one of many who had tested segregation laws. While serving in the army as a young man, he once refused to move to the back of a bus. He was court-martialed but eventually vindicated. Another protester had been Rosa Parks, who had been kicked off a Montgomery city bus when she refused to enter by the rear door.

Still another protest had come from a fifteen-year-old girl named Claudette Colvin. According to her account in a book she wrote later, she had taken a bus home on March 2, 1955. There were no white riders. She chose a seat in the middle of the bus. Within a couple of stops, two white women took seats across the aisle from Colvin in the same row. The driver ordered Colvin to get up. She stayed put.

"Why don't you get up?" a black teenage rider asked.

"She doesn't have to," said another. "Only thing you have to do is stay black and die."

"This can't go," the driver said. "I'm going to call the cops." Within minutes, Colvin was arrested and pulled from the bus.

The NAACP wanted to test the legality of this action. Then it learned that Colvin was unmarried and pregnant. Since the public would disapprove of this, Colvin wouldn't make a good symbol for the cause of desegregation. The NAACP backed off.

SOMEONE TO RALLY AROUND

By Thursday evening, December 1, 1955, Rosa Parks had put in a hard day as a tailor's assistant. The Christmas shopping season was under way, and that meant a lot of extra work. Weary, she boarded a crowded bus. She and three other black riders found seats in the no-man's land section, in the row just behind the white riders.

After several stops, all the seats on the bus had filled. One white man was left standing. The driver that evening was James Blake, the same driver who had evicted the forty-three-year-old Parks from his bus years earlier. Blake ordered the riders in Parks's row to move.

Everyone moved except Parks. She wasn't in the white section, she said. "The white section is where I say it is," Blake shot back. He threatened to have her arrested. "You may do that," she answered flatly.

Blake left the bus and called the police. They hauled Parks down to the city jail and charged her with violating segregation laws. "Why do you push us around?" Parks asked the arresting officer.

"I do not know," he responded. "But the law is the law and you're under arrest."

News of Parks's arrest traveled fast. One man who heard the news was E. D. Nixon, former head of the local chapter of the NAACP. Parks had been his secretary at the NAACP for several years. He arranged for her bail and had her released.

Parks was scheduled to appear in court the following Monday. She expected to be found guilty of violating the segregation codes and ordered to pay a fine. But Nixon didn't want Parks to quietly cooperate. When he asked her for permission to turn her case into a cause, she told him, "I'll go along with you, Mr. Nixon."

Nixon had had a lot of practice in organizing protests. Churches were often helpful. They were among the few black institutions that were independent, well organized, and relatively powerful. So Nixon called the Rev. Ralph Abernathy, a twenty-nine-year-old minister at First Baptist Church in Montgomery, asking for his help. Since the bus company depended heavily on black ridership, Nixon and Abernathy decided that a boycott of the buses made sense. In fact, the Women's Political Council (WPC) had already proposed one.

Abernathy and Nixon called a meeting of black community leaders, including sixteen prominent ministers. Martin Luther King Jr.'s name

Rosa Parks being fingerprinted after her arrest for defying segregation laws in Montgomery, Alabama, on December 1, 1955

was near the top of that list. At twenty-six, he was the new minister of Dexter Avenue Baptist Church. Abernathy had tried for nearly a year to engage King in civil rights work, but without success. Nixon called King anyway.

Meanwhile, Jo Anne Robinson, president of the local WPC, was leaping into action. Like Nixon, she also knew and respected Parks. The night of Parks's arrest, Robinson called Fred Gray, an African American attorney who worked with Nixon. She told Gray that the WPC was ready to stage a boycott of the buses.

Then she went to work making copies of a flier with a small printer that had to be hand cranked. Cranking all night, she produced thirty-five thousand copies by morning. "Don't ride the bus to work, to town, to school, or any place Monday, December 5," the flier read. Instead, people should carpool, take taxis, or walk. The flier also announced a mass meeting to be held Monday evening.

Montgomery's prominent black citizens—including the ministers Nixon had contacted—quickly met to discuss Robinson's plans. The group was split over what to do. Some urged quiet negotiations aimed at getting better treatment for African Americans within the segregated system. They walked out when others rallied behind a boycott.

The remaining leaders decided to boycott the buses for one day. They called the black-owned taxi companies in Montgomery to warn them to expect high demand on Monday. The ministers who supported the boycott preached about it from the pulpit that Sunday, when nearly all of black Montgomery was in church somewhere.

As the buses started to run on Monday morning, December 5, 1955, almost no black riders boarded. The few who did were quickly embarrassed into joining the boycott. That same morning, Rosa Parks stood trial. She was found guilty of violating segregation codes and paid a ten-dollar fine plus four dollars in court costs. She and her lawyer vowed to appeal the decision.

That afternoon the leaders of the boycott met again and named their group the Montgomery Improvement Association (MIA). They nominated the young Rev. Martin Luther King Jr. as association president since he didn't owe political favors to anyone and he could speak well. King wasn't eager to accept the nomination. But he told the group, "Somebody has to do it, and if you think I can, I will serve." He got the job.

The one-day boycott, which had been supported by nearly every African American, was clearly a success. But should it continue? The question would be resolved at the mass meeting that evening to be held at Holt Street Baptist Church. King would be a key speaker.

"This could turn into something big," he told the friend who drove him there.

A MAN NAMED KING

Holt Street Baptist Church was packed to overflowing. People stood in the aisles, in doorways, and outside, peering through windows. It took King fifteen minutes to work his way through the crowd to the pulpit.

"We are here in a general sense, because first and foremost, we are American citizens," he told his listeners. "And we are determined to apply our citizenship to the fullness of its means. But we are here in a specific sense because of the bus situation in Montgomery."

"We are determined . . . to work and fight until justice runs down like water," King told the animated crowd at Holt Street Baptist Church in Montgomery.

Some people responded as they would to a sermon, with amens and nodding heads.

"The situation is not at all new," said King. "The problem has existed over endless years. Just the other day—just last Thursday to be exact—one of the finest citizens in Montgomery—not one of the finest Negro citizens—but one of the finest citizens in Montgomery was taken from a bus and carried to jail and arrested because she refused to give up her seat to a white person." More heads nodded with yes and amen.

King said the law governing segregation on the buses was not clear. He questioned the validity of charging Parks with any crime. When he declared it was time for a change, the audience roared. "We are determined here in Montgomery," he concluded, "to work and fight until justice runs down like water and righteousness like a mighty stream." With those few words from the Bible, King managed to lay a foundation of Christian principle under a fledgling movement.

Then Rosa Parks spoke. So did Abernathy, who read the MIA's demands. The first called for courteous treatment for all on the buses. The second asked for seating on a first-come-first-served basis, after white riders had filled seats in the front and blacks in the rear. The third demand was for the hiring of black drivers for routes in black neighborhoods. Showing support for each demand, people in the audience began to sing an old hymn: "What a fellowship, / What a joy divine, / Leaning on the everlasting arms."

Everyone agreed to continue the boycott until these demands were met. The buses of Montgomery continued to roll by, empty of black faces. Boycotters walked, carpooled, or crowded into black-owned taxis, which offered reduced rates.

On Thursday, December 8, King and attorney Fred Gray met with bus company representatives and city commissioners. They restated the MIA's three demands. One commissioner, Frank Parks, would have accepted the seating arrangement as proposed. But the other commissioners protested, as did the bus company. "I don't see how

"It is more honorable to walk in dignity than ride in humiliation,"
King told bus boycotters. Protesters walked and organized carpools
as alternatives to riding segregated city buses.

we can do it within the law," said one bus company attorney. After
hours of discussion, the talks broke off with no resolution.

The boycott continued. As the weeks slipped by, the MIA organized a fleet of vehicles to ferry people to and from work. Many
churches invested in cars (dubbed "rolling churches") so they could
offer rides to protesters. White housewives secretly gave rides to their
black domestic workers. Some of these women employers continued
their support even when their husbands found out and objected.

In contrast, many boycotters faced pressure from white bosses who threatened to fire them. Police patrolled pick-up points for carpools and threatened to arrest black taxi drivers who didn't charge the same rate to all passengers. These tactics couldn't break the boycott, however. By Christmas, downtown stores were noticing a decline in sales.

Throughout December, mass meetings kept people informed and inspired. King's church hosted many meetings. People sang out in protest: "The one thing we did right, / Was the day we started to fight. / Keep your eyes on the prize, / Hold on." The bus company, feeling the lack of riders, declared itself on the verge of bankruptcy.

Ralph Abernathy **(front left)** *and Martin Luther King Jr.* **(behind Abernathy)** *joined other boycotters on the first desegregated bus in Montgomery on December 21, 1956.*

Then on January 30, 1956, a bomb exploded in King's house. King's wife and their seven-week-old daughter were home. They escaped unharmed. Two days later, another bomb exploded at E. D. Nixon's house. Again, no one was hurt.

That same day, the MIA filed a case in federal court challenging segregation on buses. The federal court ruled that segregation on the buses was illegal. Little change followed, however, since the city appealed.

As people waited for the U.S. Supreme Court to rule on the case, the bus boycotters kept up the struggle to get along without public transportation. On November 13, 1956, the Court finally affirmed the decision of the lower court. An order to desegregate the buses went into effect in December.

More than one year had passed since the arrest of Rosa Parks. During that time, Martin Luther King Jr. had become a trusted leader. "We have discovered that we can stick together for a common cause," King told people. "We have discovered a new and powerful weapon—nonviolent resistance."

The walking was over. The protesters in Montgomery had won a victory for all Americans. And a new movement had begun.

THE WALLS COME
A TUMBLIN' DOWN

Joshua fi't the battle of Jericho,
Jericho, Jericho,
Joshua fi't the battle of Jericho,
And the walls come a tumblin'
*   down.*

—Negro spiritual

Most African Americans of the 1950s knew the old spiritual "Joshua Fi't the Battle of Jericho." It tells how the Biblical hero Joshua marched his army around the seemingly invincible walled city of Jericho until its walls crumbled, leaving the city defenseless. Many African Americans, put "in their place" by laws, customs, and terrorism, saw themselves in that story. They believed God would send the walls of segregation tumbling down. The strife in Montgomery was a troubling reminder of the walls that still separated the races.

DELAY, DELAY, DELAY

The Supreme Court's ruling in *Brown v. Board of Education* should have protected the right of black students to attend integrated schools throughout 1955 and 1956. But it hadn't. The ruling was based on the Fourteenth Amendment, which had been ignored for decades. Why should anything change at this point? Segregationists vowed, "We don't want to integrate."

Riots had broken out at the University of Alabama in February 1956 when white people heard that a black student, Autherine Lucy, was registering for classes. The previously segregated university suspended Lucy, saying the suspension was for her own protection. Represented by attorney Thurgood Marshall, Lucy took the school to court and won her case. The university then expelled her for defying the school's authority.

A chief problem with *Brown* was its vague language. It clearly said that "the 'separate but equal' doctrine . . . has no place in the field of public education." The ruling did not clearly state what school districts were supposed to do about the situation, however. Some intended to comply but wanted a clearer explanation of what was expected of them. Others quietly hoped the vague wording would help them avoid integration. Still others looked to the "Southern Manifesto," a statement newly signed by southern congressmen to declare that only the states— not the federal government—could rule on segregation conflicts.

The Supreme Court had delayed nearly one year before instructing local school districts how to proceed. Even then, it said only that school districts should admit black children into public schools "on a nondiscriminatory basis." Setting no deadline, the Court directed schools to proceed "with all deliberate speed." This gave opponents plenty of time to find ways to drag out enforcement of *Brown*. As the editor of one newsletter put it, "The strategy . . . was to delay, delay, delay."

Some were frustrated by this tactic, but others praised it. As President Dwight D. Eisenhower told Congress, "If you try to go too far too fast in laws in this delicate field, . . . you are making a mistake. . . . We've got to have laws that go along with education and understanding. . . . If you go beyond that at any one time, you cause trouble."

Martin Luther King Jr., Ralph Abernathy, and sixty other civil rights advocates met in January 1957 to form a permanent organization to fight for civil rights. The Southern Christian Leadership Conference

(SCLC) opened its headquarters in Atlanta, Georgia. Its mission was nothing less than "to redeem the soul of America" through education and nonviolent action.

THE LITTLE ROCK NINE

In early 1957, Arkansas was a fairly progressive southern state. Public buses were desegregated. Blacks voted and served in elective offices. The state planned to integrate its schools as well.

In Little Rock, the state capital, the school board decided to integrate its high schools first. It selected seventeen volunteers to attend Central High, which had previously been an all-white school. The black students would start at Central on September 3, 1957.

But even in Arkansas, the integration of black students into white schools was a difficult pill to swallow. Many white people still felt outraged over the *Brown* decision. Some went to court to fight the plan to integrate Central High. When a white parent, Mrs. Clyde A. Thomason, asked for an injunction delaying integration, she testified in court that "mothers are terrified." According to her, rumors circulating in Little Rock said white teens and black teens were arming themselves with guns and knives. Mixing black and white students would result in violence.

Some people in the black community were also disconcerted. Fifteen-year-old Melba Pattillo, one of the volunteers, reported that a woman confronted her in church. "She told me I was too fancy for my britches," Melba said, "and that other people in our community would pay for my uppity need to be with white folks." Not surprisingly, some of the volunteer black students decided to back out. Melba, however, held her ground.

Despite the tension, a federal judge ruled that Little Rock must integrate. So it was a shock when Orval Faubus, governor of Arkansas, announced on September 2 that he was placing soldiers from the Arkansas National Guard around Central High to prevent black students from entering the next day. If black students tried to enter, he warned, "Blood will run in the streets."

Gloria Ray   Terrence Roberts   Melba Pattillo

Elizabeth Eckford   Ernest Green   Minnijean Brown

Jefferson Thomas   Carlotta Walls   Thelma Mothershed

THE LITTLE ROCK NINE

The Little Rock Nine, as pictured in 1957. Their challenge to segregation at Central High School in Little Rock, Arkansas, took tremendous courage and the support of their parents, ministers, and others.

The number of volunteer black students had dwindled to nine by this time. None of them were able to cross the threshold of Central High on September 3. The next day, Daisy Bates, president of the Arkansas NAACP, called eight of the students and told them to arrive at the school as a group. Bates couldn't reach the ninth student, Elizabeth Eckford.

Accompanied by their parents and ministers, the eight students found a mob of angry whites gathered outside Central High. The crowd jeered as Ernest Green, Jefferson Thomas, Terrence Roberts, Carlotta Walls, Minnijean Brown, Gloria Ray, Thelma Mothershed, and Melba Pattillo approached the school. National guardsmen blocked the entrance, and the students were forced to leave.

Since Elizabeth Eckford hadn't gotten Bates's message, she didn't know of the group's plan. She arrived alone at Central High to face the mob. People called her names, and some even threatened to lynch her. When she tried to enter the school, national guardsmen turned her away. A woman from the crowd took pity on her and led her away from the angry scene.

*Elizabeth Eckford (***wearing sunglasses***) was jeered by Hazel Bryan (***left***) when she arrived at Central High on September 4, 1957.*

National guardsmen order a heckler away from Central High School.

A federal court soon ordered the Arkansas National Guard to stop blocking the black students. Instead of ordering the guard to help the students, Governor Faubus simply removed them. With only a few policemen assigned to protect them, the black students arrived at Central High to face another belligerent crowd. "Two, four, six, eight, we don't want to integrate," chanted people in the mob. A riot broke out, and the students fled.

Finally President Eisenhower put the Arkansas national guardsmen under federal control. He also sent one thousand paratroopers from the 101st Airborne Division of the U.S. Army. "Mob rule cannot be allowed to overrule the decision of our courts," he proclaimed.

Governor Faubus remained defiant. "My fellow citizens, we are now an occupied territory," he said. "In the name of God, whom we all revere, in the name of liberty, which we hold so dear, in the name of decency, which we all cherish, what is happening in America?"

Despite his protest, the Little Rock Nine at last entered Central High on September 25. Each student was assigned a soldier escort. Even so, defiant white students continued their harassment. They spat on the newcomers, mocked them, and tripped them. Many of the black students were beaten up. Someone threw acid in Melba Pattillo's eyes. Her guard washed it out immediately, saving her eyesight.

In February 1958, a white classmate provoked Minnijean Brown, who responded by calling the girl an insulting name. Brown was expelled. The rest of the students in the Little Rock Nine completed the school year. When Ernest Green, the only senior in the group, marched across the stage at Central's graduation ceremony, most of the students did not applaud him. He said he felt a sense of triumph anyway, as he became the first black student to graduate from Central.

The following year, Governor Faubus closed all the high schools in Little Rock. Preferring no schools to integrated schools, he said the U.S. Supreme Court should "keep its cotton-picking hands off the Little Rock School Board's affairs." Eventually, this move was ruled unconstitutional. The black students returned to Central, and more black students went on to graduate.

THE GREENSBORO FOUR

Many African Americans of this era were familiar with the metaphor of the drinking gourd, first used in the days of slavery. Also called the Big Dipper, the drinking gourd is a constellation of stars, the handle of which points to the North Star. Escaping slaves used the drinking gourd to find their way as they journeyed north to freedom in states such as Ohio, Indiana, and Illinois.

The journey toward freedom of the "Greensboro Four" began when four young men were just freshmen at North Carolina A&T State University in Greensboro, North Carolina. The four were also members of the NAACP Youth Council in Greensboro.

Their story began in January 1960, when Joseph McNeil took the bus back to Greensboro after winter vacation. Getting off at the station downtown, he felt tired and hungry and thirsty. But there was no place where he could sit down to eat. As part of a deal with the NAACP, the national chain of Woolworth's stores had taken down signs saying that lunch counters were reserved for whites. Even without signs, however, a whites-only policy was in effect at the local Woolworth's and other Greensboro cafes. No one would serve McNeil.

Back at the dorm, McNeil told his roommate, David Richmond, that he was fed up. He also told Franklin McCain and Ezell Blair Jr., who both lived down the hall. The four decided to fight back—a decision McNeil later called "a down payment on manhood."

They decided to target Woolworth's. Blacks who wanted to eat at the lunch counter there had to buy food at the store's bakery or snack bar and eat it while standing. The store hired blacks to work in the kitchen but hired only white people to wait on diners.

Joseph McNeil and Franklin McCain (seated, left to right) *were members of the Greensboro Four. They are joined by two other student demonstrators to challenge segregated lunch counters.*

When the four approached the Woolworth's lunch counter on Monday, February 1, about twelve white patrons were there, taking an afternoon coffee break. The four students sat down. McCain later recalled how brazen this action seemed. "We could have had our heads split open with a night stick and [been] hauled into prison," he said.

At first the waitress and everyone else ignored them. But when the four told the waitress they wanted coffee and doughnuts, she said they couldn't be served. They didn't leave. A black employee soon arrived and lectured them on the need to follow the rules. They still didn't budge. Next the owner of the franchise, Curly Harris, ordered them out. The four still didn't move. Harris then called a police officer. The students weren't breaking the law, however, so the officer couldn't do anything. Harris decided to close the store early.

An older white woman touched McCain's shoulder. "Boys, I'm so proud of you," she said. As they said later, they knew then that they were on the right track. As the store closed and they filed out, they told Harris they would be back the next day.

That night the four met with other students and encouraged them to join the sit-in. Several volunteered, but only two showed up at Woolworth's the next day. When the local media reported the story, however, other protesters were encouraged to join the effort. Soon protesters occupied every seat at the counter. Picketers also carried signs outside Woolworth's and at a dime store half a block away. Hecklers threw some jibes, but the protest was remarkably free of violence.

The sit-in lasted for five months. In the end, the city of Greensboro created a committee that included the founder of the local Woolworth's. The store finally agreed to desegregate its counter.

Spurred by this success, sit-ins quickly spread through North Carolina and then to the rest of the nation. Stories in national newspapers such as the *New York Times* drew volunteers worldwide. Eventually, dozens of stores desegregated their counters. In April several students founded an organization, the Student Nonviolent Coordinating Committee (SNCC, or "Snick"), to coordinate the sit-ins.

FREEDOM RIDES

Meanwhile, King and the Southern Christian Leadership Conference had continued to bring civil rights issues to national attention. Many SCLC volunteers, including King, had been jailed more than once for their civil disobedience. But the SCLC was not the only group working for civil rights in this era. The Congress of Racial Equality (CORE) had been active for almost twenty years. James Leonard Farmer Jr. was CORE's dynamic director.

In February 1961, Farmer decided to test a recent U.S. Supreme Court case called *Boynton v. Virginia.* It involved Bruce Boynton, who had been refused service in a bus terminal lunchroom. The Court had ruled that segregation in public, interstate transportation facilities was illegal. Despite the ruling, most bus terminals in the South maintained separate lunchrooms, waiting areas, restrooms, and other facilities.

Farmer wanted the *Boynton* ruling enforced. He decided to send Freedom Riders—black and white—onto buses and into terminals. Black riders would use the facilities reserved for whites. White riders would use facilities for blacks. They would travel from Washington, D.C., to New Orleans, Louisiana.

Waiting rooms at bus terminals and train stations throughout the South were segregated.

On May 4, 1961, thirteen volunteers (including Farmer) boarded two buses in Washington. Black volunteers sat in front with white passengers. White volunteers sat in the back with black passengers.

At the first stops, no one bothered the riders. Then in Charlotte, North Carolina, black Freedom Rider Charles Person was jailed because he insisted on being served at a shoeshine stand, normally reserved for white clients.

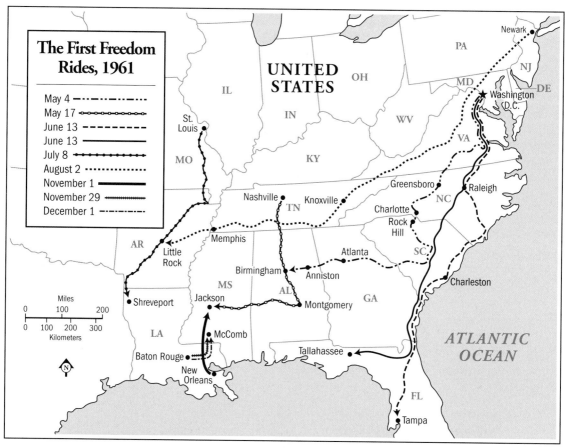

The injustice of segregation received national attention when newspapers throughout the United States featured the Freedom Rides. One national news service published a map like this one along with an article.

News of the Freedom Riders reached Rock Hill, South Carolina, ahead of the buses. By the time the first bus arrived, an angry crowd had gathered at the terminal. Freedom Riders John Lewis and Albert Bigelow were badly beaten. Then a police officer intervened, and the Freedom Riders entered the waiting area with no more problems.

Days later in Anniston, Alabama, a mob of more than two hundred whites threatened the riders with clubs and bricks. Someone threw a firebomb and set the bus ablaze. The mob pulled back only when a policeman pulled his revolver.

Ahead of the riders lay Birmingham, Alabama. Within the past six years, Birmingham had been the site of eighteen unsolved bombings in black neighborhoods. Some people called the city "Bombingham." When the Freedom Riders arrived, no police were on hand. Angry whites swarmed the bus, pulled the Freedom Riders out, and beat, kicked, and clubbed them. The mob then destroyed the bus with a firebomb. Farmer had the Freedom Riders flown to New Orleans to safety and as a symbolic end to their ride.

CORE refused to drop the Freedom Rides, however. More volunteers arrived in Birmingham, boarded buses, and continued on. In Montgomery, Alabama, another angry mob met the riders. At stops in Mississippi, some Freedom Riders were thrown into jail.

As the summer wore on, Freedom Riders took buses through the states of Alabama, Arkansas, Florida, Georgia, Kentucky, Louisiana, Mississippi, North Carolina, South Carolina, Tennessee, and Virginia. Their stubborn persistence generated publicity for the cause. As more volunteers stepped forward, Freedom Riders started showing up not only in bus stations but also in train stations and at airports throughout the South.

Their efforts paid off with a significant triumph that fall. The Interstate Commerce Commission issued new rules enforcing integration in transportation facilities. By insisting on their rights, the Freedom Riders had blasted another hole in the segregation wall.

THE FIRES OF FRUSTRATION AND DISCORD

I'm gonna tell my Lord
When I get home,
I'm gonna tell my Lord
When I get home,
Just how long you've
Been treating me wrong.
                —song of the American
                        civil rights movement

At the beginning of 1963, as Martin Luther King Jr. turned thirty-five, he was recovering from what newspapers were calling "the most stunning defeat" of his career. The Southern Christian Leadership Conference had spent a year in Albany, Georgia, but had failed to accomplish most of its goals. Albany city officials had gone to great lengths to avoid integrating city facilities, even closing the parks. The schools remained segregated. King was depressed.

King went to Birmingham that spring at the invitation of Fred Shuttlesworth, pastor of Bethel Baptist Church. A founding member of the SCLC, Shuttlesworth wanted Birmingham lunch counters and other businesses to integrate.

People in the black community in Birmingham seemed ready to fight Birmingham's deeply rooted history of segregation. To do so, however, they would have to face the threat of violence that had long hung over the city. They also faced an iron-willed police commissioner, Eugene "Bull" Connors, who fiercely opposed desegregation.

Led by Shuttlesworth and King, community members launched their demonstration on April 3, 1963. The demonstrators sat in at segregated lunch counters and picketed shopping areas. As anticipated, they were arrested and jailed by Connors and his men.

Three days later, the ongoing protest grew violent. A crowd of protesters and other onlookers watched, horrified, as police dogs attacked Leroy Allen, a nineteen-year-old protester.

To preserve the peace, Judge W. A. Jenkins issued an injunction barring further protests. The injunction didn't surprise Shuttlesworth, King, or other SCLC leaders. They were surprised, however, when many members of the black community and some liberal whites supported it.

King wasn't quite sure what to do about this. He didn't want the failure in Albany to be repeated in Birmingham. He and other SCLC members discussed options for hours. Then King abruptly rose and went into the next room. Everyone was confused until he emerged a few minutes later. He had changed into blue jeans, his "go to jail" clothes.

"Look, I don't know what to do," King said. "I just know that something has got to change in Birmingham. I don't know if I can raise money to get people out of jail. I do know that I can go to jail with them."

April 12 was Good Friday, one of the most important days on the Christian calendar. Ordinarily King would have spent the day preparing an Easter sermon on the resurrection of Jesus. Instead, in defiance of Judge Jenkins's order, he led a march toward City Hall. He was quickly arrested, jailed, and placed in solitary confinement.

On the following Monday, a local paper published an open letter written by eight white religious leaders. They called King to task for not waiting until city officials had had a chance to work things out.

Ralph Abernathy (left) *and Martin Luther King Jr.* (right) *were arrested on April 12, 1963, for leading a civil rights march in Birmingham, Alabama, in defiance of a court order.*

"Frankly," he wrote in response, "I have yet to engage in a direct action campaign that was well timed in the view of those who have not suffered unduly from the disease of segregation. For years now I have heard the word 'Wait!' It rings in the ear of every Negro with piercing familiarity. This 'Wait' has almost always meant 'Never.' We must come to see . . . that 'justice too long delayed is justice denied.'" Scrawled in a cramped cell, this "letter from a Birmingham jail" came to be considered one of the greatest documents of the century. King sat in jail for eight long days.

THE CHILDREN OF BIRMINGHAM

In the meantime, most of the demonstrators had returned to work. So the children of Birmingham, who didn't have to work, took up the cause. On May 2, 1963, one thousand youngsters stayed out of school and went to the Sixteenth Street Baptist Church to prepare for a protest march. Bull Connors ordered police and police vans to wait near the site. The young protesters left the church anyway, marching in groups of about fifty at a time. As they marched, they sang, "I'm on my way, / to freedom land. / I asked mother, / come go with me. / If my mother don't go, / I'll go anyhow. / I'm on my way, oh, Lord, / to freedom land." Police arrested one group after another. By the end of the day, more than nine hundred youngsters had been ordered into police vans and taken to jail.

More young marchers gathered the next day. The jails were full. Connors was determined not to let the march proceed, so he directed police to threaten the marchers with clubs and to set police dogs on the marchers. Reporters' cameras caught the scene in unflinching detail as Connors next turned to his firefighters and ordered them to turn on

Birmingham police arrested so many children on May 2, 1963, that they had to haul them to jail in school buses as well as in police vans. The youngsters were aged six to eighteen.

their hoses. Water with enough pressure to tear the bark from trees blasted toward the young marchers. It tossed some of them into the air and slammed others against walls. Little girls rolled down the street like rag dolls. Shuttlesworth was injured so badly that he was hospitalized.

Even antagonists were surprised by this sight. TV stations and newspapers carried the story around the United States and abroad, triggering widespread outrage.

George Wallace, governor of Alabama, dismissed the criticism, especially from other nations. According to Wallace, "The average man in Africa and Asia doesn't even know where he is, much less where Alabama is."

On May 3, 1963, Birmingham police used high-pressure fire hoses and police dogs against civil rights marchers.

Tension in the city was unbearably high, but that didn't stop the children. On the following Monday, comedian and activist Dick Gregory joined them for further demonstrations. The following day, violence broke out between blacks and whites in the downtown business district.

The threat to their businesses finally forced white business leaders to talk to SCLC leaders. Within a few days, the two sides had hammered out a plan to desegregate downtown businesses. Owners would open lunch counters to all. They would remove signs designating separate fitting rooms and bathrooms for blacks and whites. They would hire more blacks to work downtown. The SCLC had the victory it needed.

Little more than a day after things seemed settled, a bomb exploded outside a hotel room where King was staying. Some witnesses later claimed that the Ku Klux Klan was responsible. King was not there at the time, and no one was injured. But blacks around the city rioted in reaction, and police moved in and began beating some people. Forty people were injured, and several buildings were destroyed by fire.

On June 11, 1963, President John F. Kennedy spoke to a troubled nation. "The fires of frustration and discord are burning in every city, North and South," he said. "Where legal remedies are not at hand, redress is sought in the street, in demonstrations, parades, and protests which create tensions and threaten violence and threaten lives." By pointing out the context of black reaction, Kennedy was making the strongest stand on race relations that he had ever made.

THE HIGH PRICE OF FREEDOM

The night Kennedy spoke, Myrtle Evers was watching him on television. Her children were asleep, and she was listening with keen interest to what the president had to say. She was the wife of Medgar Evers, field secretary for the NAACP in Mississippi. "It is not enough to pin the blame on others, to say that this is a problem of one section of the country or another," Kennedy said. "A great change is at hand and our task, our obligation is to make change peaceful and constructive for all.

Those who do nothing are inviting shame as well as violence. Those who act boldly are recognizing right as well as reality."

Evers was pleasantly surprised. Like so many in the black community, she had supported Kennedy but was privately disappointed over his seeming lack of commitment to civil rights. Finally, it seemed, her faith in Kennedy was justified. She wondered if her husband was listening, perhaps over the radio in his car. As she waited to share the good news with him, she drifted off to sleep.

Medgar Evers's focus was registration of black voters. Mississippi used a variety of tactics to keep blacks off the voting rolls. For example, officials gave black applicants impossible poll tests and charged expensive poll taxes. Sometimes would-be black voters were threatened or even lynched. Working with the NAACP, Evers chronicled the torture, mutilation, and murder of victims throughout the region. A few weeks before President Kennedy's remarkable speech, someone had thrown a bomb into Evers's garage. No one had been injured.

Just before midnight and hours after Kennedy's speech ended, Myrtle Evers awakened to the sound of a car in the driveway. She listened carefully, knowing violence was a constant threat. With relief, she recognized the sound of Medgar's car. The car door opened and slammed shut with a familiar thud. Medgar was home.

Then without warning came the unmistakable report of a single blast from a high-powered rifle. Awakened, the Evers children hit the floor as their father had taught them. Myrtle ran to the front door and threw it open. She saw her husband on the ground, crawling toward her. A trail of blood marked his progress. He had been shot in the back. He died within the hour, at the age of thirty-seven. Later, he was buried in Arlington National Cemetery in the nation's capital with full military honors.

Byron de la Beckwith, a white man from Greenwood, Mississippi, was later charged with Evers's murder. Although de la Beckwith's fingerprints were the only ones found on the murder weapon, he wasn't convicted. "We view this as a cold, brutal, deliberate killing in . . . the

The funeral procession for NAACP leader Medgar Evers in 1963

most savage, the most uncivilized state in the entire fifty states," said Roy Wilkins, executive director of the NAACP.

THE MARCH ON WASHINGTON

Evers's murder intensified the sense of urgency felt by many in the movement. Two decades earlier, union organizer Asa Philip Randolph had urged a march on Washington. The time had finally come for Americans to gather on behalf of civil rights.

Movement leaders approached President Kennedy with the idea. He was uncomfortable with allowing masses of people to demonstrate in Washington. Trying to squelch the march, he invited march organizers to the White House. They were unmoved by his arguments. The march would include both blacks and whites, and they believed it could draw the nation together. As Randolph said, "This civil rights revolution is not confined to the Negroes. . . . Our white allies know that they cannot be free while we are not."

Determined to proceed, organizers set a date of August 28, 1963, for the march. Randolph served as chairperson. Expert organizer Bayard Rustin orchestrated the logistics. Almost every civil rights group would participate, including the NAACP, SNCC, CORE, the SCLC, and the Nation of Islam, a black separatist group that was usually critical of working with whites.

All these groups differed about some things, but the planning for this march drew them together. Only one issue seemed to threaten their unity. Speakers were asked to let Kennedy staff members see drafts of their speeches. Kennedy's staff thought the speech of SNCC's John Lewis (who had been a Freedom Rider in 1961) painted them in a negative light. "Where is the political party that will make it unnecessary to march on Washington?" the speech asked. Lewis balked at changing these lines, and tension mounted. When Randolph himself asked for a change, however, Lewis relented.

August 28, 1963, was an unforgettable day. More than two hundred thousand people gathered at the Capitol Mall. Stars such as

"I have a dream," Martin Luther King Jr. told the crowd of more than two hundred thousand gathered for the March on Washington.

Dick Gregory and Marlon Brando rubbed shoulders with sharecroppers from Mississippi and foundry workers from northern ghettos.

Martin Luther King Jr. was fresh from Birmingham. When he stepped to the podium, he spoke with renewed hope. "I have a dream," he told listeners. He spoke of a nation awakening from the nightmare of racial discrimination, ready to deliver the promises of the Constitution. By day's end, his challenge to Americans to "let freedom ring" seemed possible.

Most Americans knew nothing of the controversies behind this event. For them, the March on Washington was a defining moment in a unified civil rights movement. As President Kennedy later told reporters, "If one was American and believed in the equality of man, on August 28, 1963, there was no other place to be."

"What counted most," said march organizer Bayard Rustin, "was the pledge of a quarter of a million Americans, black and white, to carry the civil rights revolution into the streets."

Then on Sunday morning, September 15, Birmingham exploded again. A bomb rocked the Sixteenth Street Baptist Church just as its African American members were gathering for the Sunday morning service. According to the news source United Press International (UPI), "The bomb apparently went off in an unoccupied basement room and blew down the wall, sending stone and debris flying like shrapnel into a room where children were assembling." In addition, UPI reported:

> Dozens of survivors, their faces dripping with blood from the glass that flew out of the church's stained glass windows, staggered around the building in a cloud of white dust raised by the explosion. The blast crushed two nearby cars like toys and blew out windows blocks away.

Some of the children who had marched in Birmingham were in the church at the time. Fifteen people were injured. Four young girls were killed. At their funeral, people sang "We Shall Overcome." As they sang, they must have wondered whether freedom could dampen the fires of frustration and discord anytime soon.

ON MY WAY

I'm on my way to freedom land.
I asked mother, come go with me.
If my mother don't go,
I'll go anyhow.
I'm on my way, oh, Lord,
To freedom land.
　　　　　—song of the American
　　　　　　　civil rights movement

The chairs sat empty behind the neat rows of desks, and an eerie silence hung in the room. North Division High School in Milwaukee, Wisconsin, normally bustled with hundreds of students. It shouldn't have been so quiet on a Monday morning. Teacher Bessie Jones sat alone, thinking up something to do during the time she usually spent teaching.

This scene was repeated in many schools around Milwaukee on May 18, 1964. An estimated 14,127 of the city's inner-city students (nearly 60 percent of them) were absent. Another 10,000 students from other parts of the district also did not show up for school.

Superintendent of schools Harold Vincent claimed that the missing students were ill. Many of the supposedly ill students showed up, however, at temporary classrooms in thirty locations around the city.

Volunteers had set up these makeshift Freedom Schools in preparation for a massive, city-wide boycott of the schools.

One Freedom School was located in the rectory at Saint Boniface Catholic Church. The room was packed. Young voices mingled with those of adults, and a song filled the air: "Ain't gonna let nobody / Turn me round. / Ain't gonna let no school board / Turn me round. / Keep on walkin', / Keep on marchin', / Headin' for the freedom land."

DE FACTO

Milwaukee was a city of about seven hundred thousand in 1964. Nearly 10 percent of its people were African American. Many of them had recently migrated to Milwaukee from the South. Others were the children or grandchildren of earlier generations who had migrated there, arriving in a steady stream since the 1920s, looking for jobs and a better life.

In Milwaukee, they found no obvious discrimination—no grisly lynchings, no signs designating water fountains for "whites" or "coloreds." No local laws forced black youngsters into segregated schools. Yet most of the city's schools seemed defined by color.

One reason was that many African Americans—especially newly arrived immigrants—were largely unskilled. Poorly paid in their jobs, they could afford only the poorest housing. Most (more than 80 percent of Milwaukee's African Americans) crowded into one area, the city's inner core. Meanwhile, many better-paid white workers and their families moved to the suburbs.

With black families living near one another in the inner city, it seemed that their children just happened to end up at the same schools. In fact, Milwaukee's inner-city schools had student bodies that were 95 percent black. Many other schools in Milwaukee had no black students at all. Perhaps students were not being segregated on purpose. The effect was the same, however.

Worse, many people charged that schools with black students were inferior. Rumors flew that Roosevelt Junior High School and

Wilbur Wright Junior High School had textbooks, classrooms, shop equipment, and libraries far inferior to those in junior highs with white student bodies.

One local attorney, Lloyd Barbee, served as president of the Wisconsin NAACP. Concerned about the seeming segregation, he called Wisconsin's state superintendent of public instruction early in 1963. Barbee charged that Milwaukee's schools reflected "de facto" (as a point of fact) segregation. The idea of de facto segregation was new. In the South, segregation had been required by state and local laws and codes.

Superintendent Angus Rothwell regretted that he couldn't help. He couldn't act to change the situation unless he had proof of illegal segregation. He ordered an investigation, then called Barbee in September 1963 with the findings. Milwaukee school officials claimed they were doing nothing to cause the pattern of segregation.

The following March, Barbee and other civil rights activists formed a new organization to work for change. The Milwaukee United School Integration Committee (MUSIC) decided to carry out its own investigation. MUSIC volunteers toured local schools to check out facilities and school policies (for example, some people charged that students at Roosevelt Junior High were punished by being paddled). Disturbed by what it found, MUSIC organized the May 18 school boycott in protest.

The more MUSIC studied the pattern of de facto segregation, the more its members began to believe that segregation was partly intended. For example, the school board had drawn some school boundary lines between white neighborhoods and black neighborhoods. The board allowed white students to transfer out of black schools but seldom allowed black students to do so. The board hired African American teachers and staff for black schools, but not for white schools.

The school board would not budge, so students undertook another boycott that October. In addition, Lloyd Barbee served as lawyer for

This neighborhood was typical of poor housing for African Americans in Milwaukee and elsewhere. Poor neighborhoods often had inferior schools.

a class action desegregation lawsuit against the school district. Some of the parents and students who joined the lawsuit were white—the first time that whites had joined a school segregation complaint.

All the complaints against Milwaukee schools had to be proven. Lloyd Barbee could not have known in October 1965 that the case would drag on and on as MUSIC combed through school records, polled families, and assembled statistics. Gathering evidence took the next fifteen years.

Sadly, the situation in Milwaukee was not unique. Throughout the 1960s, fairness in schools and housing, North and South, continued to seem maddeningly out of reach.

THE SUMMER OF '64

The Mississippi Delta, with its gently rolling hills and mild climate, is one of the most beautiful regions in the country. In the early 1960s, about 45 percent of the people there were black—the highest percentage of any state. Few of those people were professionals. Most worked as laborers in conditions that had changed little since the days of slavery. Only 5 percent were registered to vote in these years.

Many African Americans had already abandoned Mississippi to migrate north. But others had refused to give up the home of their ancestors. They lived their lives like the song they sang in church: "We shall not be moved. / Just like a tree planted by the water, / We shall not be moved." Determined to make Mississippi a place where blacks could better live their lives through voting, a diverse group came together in what was called the Mississippi Freedom Movement.

The protests of this movement got under way in the summer of 1964, less than a year after the March on Washington. They were mostly organized by the Council of Federated Organizations (COFO), a confederation of civil rights organizations including the NAACP, SCLC, CORE, and SNCC. The goal was not only to register blacks to vote but also to sign them up for the Mississippi Freedom Democratic Party (MFDP). If enough blacks registered and voted with the MFDP as a block, they could challenge the largely white Democratic Party in Mississippi by demanding representatives of their own at the Democratic state convention that year.

To power the voter registration drive, COFO recruited volunteers at northern colleges. Eight hundred of these volunteers met in Oxford, Ohio, in early June. SNCC leaders (including Cleave Sellers, Bob Moses, and James Forman) put the volunteers through rigorous training in nonviolent-protest methods.

Unlike many others in the civil rights movement, many of these student recruits were white. And they were from privileged backgrounds. Their presence in Mississippi was bound to attract media attention. As one student from Harvard put it, "If a young black from Mississippi were to get arrested or put in jail, that would be that. But if one of us [white students from wealthy families] got put in jail, then it'd be senator so-and-so on the phone, congressman so-and-so on the phone, the *New York Times* calling."

Oddly enough, the upper-class white volunteers often acted as if they felt superior to the black volunteers, who were less well educated and came from less affluent backgrounds. The irony that blacks were "less important" than whites even within the civil rights movement led to mistrust on both sides.

African Americans line up to cast their ballots in rural Alabama. SNCC volunteers worked hard during the summer of 1964 to encourage black voter registration in the South.

This FBI poster asks for information on the location of (left to right) *Andrew Goodman, James Chaney, and Michael Schwerner.*

When the first handful of volunteers headed south, however, they encountered even worse attitudes about blacks and voting. As one southern judge said, "I don't want the Negro as I have known him . . . to control the government under which I live."

On June 21, three of the volunteers—Andrew Goodman, James Chaney, and Michael Schwerner—were arrested in Mississippi for speeding after investigating a church bombing. The three men (two white and one black) were released, but then they disappeared.

Hearing this news, the SNCC trainers in Ohio suspected the three were dead. Three hundred volunteers were ready to head south to start the voter registration effort. Bob Moses told them, "Some of you in this room might not return from Mississippi," he said. "And you shouldn't feel you have to go." He paused. "But you have to go, too.

I don't want to have to put you at risk this way, but I have to put you at risk. The danger is real. All I can say is that I'll be there with you."

No one stirred. Then a woman stood and sang, "They say that freedom is a constant struggle, / They say that freedom is a constant struggle, / Oh Lord, we been strugglin' so long, / We must be free." The others took up the song, resolved to commit to the struggle.

The students arrived in force in Mississippi by early July. They started Freedom Schools, teaching youngsters who didn't have adequate schooling. The students also held political rallies or fanned out, registering blacks to vote and signing them up for the MFDP.

The state of Mississippi had armed itself for this invasion. A large number of new police recruits were heavily armed and clad in riot gear. Police made more than one thousand arrests. There were church bombings, thirty-five shootings, and eighty beatings of movement people by the Klu Klux Klan and other angry whites.

Police arrested more than one thousand civil rights activists for illegal protests the summer of 1964.

Flanked by civil rights supporters, President Lyndon Johnson signs the Civil Rights Act of 1964 on July 19.

By this time, the civil rights movement had become a critical, national issue. National leaders were ready to make major shifts in policy. The movement had a major victory when President Lyndon Johnson signed the Civil Rights Act of 1964. It mandated equal access to all public places, and it outlawed job discrimination across the country. "We have talked long enough in this country about rights," Johnson said in a televised speech. "We have talked for one hundred years or more. It is time now to write the next chapter—and to write it in books of law."

On August 4, the bodies of Goodman, Chaney, and Schwerner were found. The men had been buried on a Mississippi farm near their abandoned car, which had been discovered six weeks earlier. Goodman and Schwerner had been shot. Chaney had obviously been beaten before being killed. Jurors later convicted seven people for conspiracy and murder. Among them were local law enforcement officials and members of the Ku Klux Klan.

"SICK AND TIRED"

Meanwhile, SNCC volunteers signed up sixty thousand black and white members for the Mississippi Freedom Democratic Party. The party's state convention had included only white delegates. In response, MFDP selected sixty-eight delegates of its own.

These delegates (sixty-four of them black, four of them white) traveled to the Democratic Party's national convention in Atlantic City, New Jersey, to challenge and unseat the regular delegates. MFDP delegate Fanny Lou Hamer got people's attention when she spoke to the packed room at the convention. The granddaughter of slaves and the youngest of twenty children in a family of sharecroppers, she was not well educated. But she spoke with passion and clarity.

"I'm sick and tired of being sick and tired," she told everyone. "If the [Mississippi] Freedom Democratic Party is not seated now, I question America. Is this America, the land of the free and the home of the brave? Where we have to sleep with our phones off the hook, because our lives are threatened daily?" Hamer's remarks made such a strong impression that they aired that day on the national nightly news.

In the end, the Democratic Party would not unseat the official party delegates from Mississippi. The MFDP delegates were disappointed, but they knew they had paved the way for greater participation by blacks and other minorities in the Democratic Party.

SELMA, BLOODY SUNDAY

In December 1964, Martin Luther King Jr. was awarded the Nobel Peace Prize. *Time* magazine named him "Man of the Year." These honors and national policy shifts seemed to confirm that blacks were emerging from second-class citizenship.

Even so, the "fires of frustration and discord" smoldered within the civil rights movement and throughout the nation. In February 1965 in Harlem, New York, three members of the Nation of Islam assassinated their former leader Malcolm X, who had left the group.

Down in Alabama, SNCC had targeted Selma for a voter registration campaign. Half of the people in Dallas County (which included Selma) were black. Only 1 percent of them were registered to vote. In January 1965, SNCC asked King and other SCLC leaders for help.

The two organizations began working together. One night in February, angry white onlookers charged a group of SNCC and SCLC protesters who were marching on the town of Marion, near Selma. When marcher Jim Jackson, who was with his mother, tried to shield her from attacks, he was shot at point blank range by a state trooper. Jackson died eight days later.

SNCC considered taking up arms. Violence went against the teachings of the SCLC, however. Tension grew between the two groups. Instead of splitting, they decided to march to the state capitol in Montgomery. Led by John Lewis and Hosea Williams of SNCC, about six hundred demonstrators would walk the sixty-some miles.

Governor George Wallace banned further marches. Marchers assembled anyway on Sunday, March 7, at Brown Chapel in Selma. All was quiet as they began walking. At the outskirts of the city, however, they ran into a wall of Alabama state troopers. Dispatched by Wallace, the troopers charged into the marchers, billy clubs swinging and clouds of tear gas billowing around them. Many of the protesters were injured. When film of this scene was aired on national television, the encounter was dubbed Bloody Sunday.

Alabama state troopers confront protesters outside of Selma. "The tear gas burned our eyes," one protester later recalled.

Americans were horrified. "Shame on you George Wallace...," said Ralph Yarborough, a Democratic senator from Texas. "This is not the American way."

Plans for a second march were quickly announced, and many politicians and clergymen, including James Reeb of Boston, flew to Selma. On March 8, one day after Reeb's arrival, white thugs attacked him.

Meanwhile, a local court had issued an injunction (ruling) against the march. King assured those who had gathered in Selma that he would fight for the right to proceed. "We've gone too far now to turn back," he explained. Two thousand protesters gathered at Brown Chapel on March 9 and began to march. Again they found troopers at the city's outskirts. This time, King urged the marchers to kneel and pray. When they rose, he turned them around and led them back to the church. Two days later, James Reeb died.

SNCC members felt betrayed by King's apparent passivity. But King asked everyone to be patient and stay together a few days longer. A federal judge then ruled that the demonstrators had a right to march. President Johnson federalized Alabama's National Guard, ordering them to protect the marchers.

On March 21, twenty-five hundred marchers finally left Selma on the long road to Montgomery. Blacks and whites walked together. Joined by protesters along the way, they were twenty-five thousand strong when they reached the state capitol five days later. National news stories made them a vivid symbol of the right to vote regardless of race.

Many historians credit the Selma marchers with setting the stage for passage of the Voting Rights Act of 1965, signed by President Johnson on August 6. "This cause must be our cause too," Johnson said. "All of us... must overcome the crippling legacy of bigotry and injustice. And we shall overcome." The new law said no state could use unfair tests—or other methods—to keep African Americans from voting. It appeared as if nonviolence had proven itself.

The victory was short-lived, however. SNCC members, younger and more radical than the members of the SCLC, had grown

Nonviolent protests of racism, such as the march on Selma, Alabama **(left)**, *contrasted sharply with riots in Watts, California* **(right)**, *and other cities as frustration erupted into anger during 1965.*

restless and resentful. They seemed to hear the words of another old spiritual: "God gave Noah, / The rainbow sign, / No more water, / Fire next time." Some were attracted to the Nation of Islam, which taught that blacks would never achieve freedom until they established a separate nation and followed their version of the Islamic faith. The Nation's leaders preached that nonviolent methods could never be effective against a violent white society.

FIRE NEXT TIME

The fire struck first in Watts, California, on August 11, 1965. As part of Los Angeles County, this West Coast community was thought to be free of the ills troubling the South. But African Americans in Watts earned poor wages and lived in overcrowded neighborhoods. Resentment smoldered beneath the surface. That August day, two policemen stopped an African American driver on suspicion of being drunk. When one officer hit an innocent onlooker with his police baton, witnesses were outraged. Anger over police mistreatment burst forth as residents began rioting and looting. After four days of turmoil, thirty-four people were dead and hundreds were injured. A similar rage smoldered in Detroit, Michigan; Milwaukee, Wisconsin; Newark, New Jersey; and other cities. It seemed nearly every corner of the country held a time bomb waiting to explode.

THE MARCH AGAINST FEAR

On June 5, 1966, James Meredith began walking from Memphis, Tennessee, to Jackson, Mississippi—a distance of 220 miles. He had chosen one of the most dangerous routes in the United States for a black man. But after all, he had been the first black student ever to attend the University of Mississippi. His presence had sparked riots when he had enrolled four years earlier. In fact, Mississippi was

James Meredith was ambushed by a sniper while making a long-distance walk in a personal statement of protest and courage. He later recovered.

Stokeley Carmichael **(center)**, ***who succeeded John Lewis as head of SNCC in 1966, often told listeners, "We need power."***

consistently hostile toward any change in race relations. Black residents lived in a state of constant terror. Meredith was determined to free people from that paralyzing fear.

The first day of his walk went smoothly. On the second day, however, Meredith was ambushed and shot in the back. He collapsed along the roadside. His companions had him rushed to a Memphis hospital.

The major civil rights organizations vowed to continue Meredith's march, beginning at the point he had been gunned down. Hundreds of people gathered there. Martin Luther King Jr. urged them to seek a nonviolent solution. But the new president of SNCC, Stokeley Carmichael, declared, "I'm not going to beg the white man for anything that I deserve. We need power."

The marchers began winding their way through the Mississippi countryside. Like earlier marchers, they sang. But this time, their songs were defiant. "Freedom got a shotgun, / Freedom got a shotgun, / You know freedom gonna shoot it / At these segregated bigots."

As the march wound its way through the Mississippi countryside, Carmichael pounded home the need for power. "Become so strong they'll be afraid to mess with us," he told marchers. He encouraged whites in the group to work separately, to band with other whites in working against racism. Throughout the twenty-two days of the march, Carmichael and SNCC leaders encouraged people along the way to register to vote.

In many ways, the march was a success, and Meredith felt well enough to join the group in Jackson. Prompted in part by the march, four thousand blacks registered to vote. But the civil rights movement would never be the same. The old partnership of middle-class blacks, liberal whites, and poor blacks was being replaced with the steely vision that Carmichael dubbed Black Power.

SEEN THE PROMISED LAND

The SCLC remained committed to nonviolence. It headed to Chicago for Freedom Sunday, July 10, 1966. There, King led five thousand marchers in a protest against unequal employment, education, and housing. The group wound through downtown Chicago and stopped at City Hall. King demanded "redress of legitimate grievances." In a dramatic gesture, he tacked the group's demands to the door at City Hall.

When Mayor Richard Daly did little to address black concerns, King tried to prompt action with another march. This time he focused on a Chicago suburb that excluded blacks. Twelve hundred police stood by as King led a large, peaceful group of marchers into the segregated suburb. Suddenly the march was met by an angry mob of about five thousand whites. The men, women, and children in the mob held signs painted with swastikas—the symbol of Hitler's anti-Jewish Germany. They shouted racial slurs at the marchers and threw rocks and firecrackers at them. Police could barely restrain the mob from beating the marchers.

King left Chicago in frustration. But he had discovered a new focus. In the 1950s, the civil rights movement had pressed to end separate and unequal treatment under the law, particularly in public places. It had fought for voting rights. One by one, unfair laws had been challenged and changed. But no law could ever force American society to make blacks fully equal citizens. Poverty was crippling blacks as much as segregation once had.

This problem of economics is what led King to take up the cause of the sanitation workers in Memphis, Tennessee, in April 1968. These black workers were demanding higher wages and an end to mistreatment by white supervisors. When King arrived in Memphis, he checked into a room at the Lorraine Motel.

Jesse L. Jackson (left) *and Ralph Abernathy* (right) *with Martin Luther King Jr.* (center) *at the Lorraine Motel in Memphis, Tennessee, in April 1968*

When he spoke at the Bishop Charles Mason Temple on April 3, he talked about the threat of violence. "Like anyone, I would like to live a long life," he said. "Longevity has its place. But I'm not concerned about that now. I just want to do God's will. And he's allowed me to go up to the mountain. And I've looked over. And I've seen the Promised Land. I may not get there with you. But I want you to know tonight, I'm not worried about anything. I'm not fearing any man. Mine eyes have seen the glory of the coming of the Lord." The next day, April 4, 1968, on the balcony outside King's room at the motel, he was shot by an unseen gunman.

GATHERING STORM

It was a quiet spring night. At a bar on the east side of Cleveland, Ohio, the usual crowd was sipping drinks, talking, and listening to the music of a local jazz band.

Suddenly the streets erupted with the scream of sirens, the flash of lights, and the rumble of emergency vehicles. The band continued playing, but something had changed. The patrons eyed one another quizzically as talk shifted to speculation about what was going on outside.

"Must be an awful big fire," one man said. He probably meant to sound matter-of-fact, but an unspoken fear filled his voice. No single fire could cause that commotion. Were people rioting, as they had in Watts, Detroit, and Milwaukee?

For a few tense minutes, the band played and the patrons waited to find out what was happening. Then a man in his twenties burst into the club shouting, "They shot Martin Luther King!"

No one who thought about it should have been surprised. King had survived earlier attempts on his life. And there had been many other casualties in the race wars. Still, people were stunned. The music stopped. Conversation stopped. People could not form the words to express their grief, bewilderment, and rage. In the silence, they wondered whether all the progress that had been made would be undone. Far to the south, King lay dying, the victim of an assassin's bullet.

Countless Americans revered Martin Luther King Jr. as a national hero and deeply mourned his death.

SOLVING THE AMERICAN PROBLEM

There is no Negro problem. There is no southern problem. There is no northern problem. There is only an American problem.
  —President Lyndon B. Johnson
          March 15, 1965

Millions around the world mourned the loss of Martin Luther King Jr. His death triggered a profound change in the civil rights movement. "The death of Dr. King signals the end of an era and the beginning of a terrible and bloody [new] chapter," wrote black activist Eldridge Cleaver. And, in fact, people's anger led to riots in many cities. The struggle to achieve the movement's goals would never be the same.

FRAGMENTATION

Within a year of King's death, the fragile partnership that had made the movement possible began to dissolve. Many younger blacks drifted away. Like Eldridge Cleaver, they believed the fight for civil rights could not be won in partnership with whites. "Our basic need is to reclaim . . . our identity . . . ," Stokeley Carmichael wrote in his book *Black Power.* "We will have to struggle for ourselves." He urged readers not to adopt the goal of the civil rights movement—an equal share in American society. What was needed was a fundamental change in that society.

Not surprisingly, white supporters of the movement pulled back. Some put their energy into protesting American involvement in the Vietnam War. Using the techniques of the civil rights movement, they organized marches and sit-ins against the war.

The Black Panther Party, organized in California after the Watts riots, put the goal of black separatism into sharp focus. Leaders such as Huey Newton, Bobby Seals, and Eldridge Cleaver demanded that blacks control their own politics, economics, and education. These goals could not be won through nonviolence alone. According to Cleaver, "Black people are no longer interested in . . . negotiating. . . . Their only interest now is in being able to summon up whatever it will take to . . . force Babylon [white-controlled society] to let the black people go."

Opposite, *King's widow, Coretta Scott King.* **Above,** *Black Panthers raise their fists in the Black Power gesture, asserting unity and demanding fundamental change.*

Calling for an armed revolution, militant blacks often clashed with police. Black Panther leader Huey Newton was jailed for killing a police officer. His case launched a nationwide crackdown on radical black organizations. One police raid in Chicago ended in the deaths of two Black Panthers.

Still more heirs to civil rights activism also declared that blacks should control their own destiny. But the cultural nationalists, as they were called, did not preach armed struggle as the way to achieve that control. Instead they maintained the civil rights movement's commitment to nonviolence. They pushed black art as a way to teach others black history and culture. They celebrated black beauty. Their ranks included writer James Baldwin; photographer Gordon Parks; dancers Alvin Ailey and Katherine Dunham; and musicians John Coltrane, Charles Mingus, and Rahsan Roland Kirk, among many others.

Perhaps the best-known new leader was the charismatic Rev. Jesse L. Jackson. He had been part of King's inner circle of advisers. An ordained Baptist minister, Jackson served as president of SCLC from 1967 to 1971. He left to establish the Chicago-based People United to Save Humanity (Operation PUSH). In the following years, this group advocated economic justice, demanding fair hiring practices and promotions and pushing for more opportunities for blacks to establish their own businesses.

AFFIRMATIVE ACTION

Jackson also played a role in "affirmative action" efforts. The phrase had been coined by President John F. Kennedy in a 1961 executive order. The order said federal contractors should take affirmative action to ensure that job applicants and employees be treated without regard to their race, creed, or national origin.

Affirmative action programs were established in part to make more jobs available to minorities. Many of these programs required cities and counties to ensure that a certain percentage of their workers were members of minority groups (such as blacks and Hispanics).

Local governments were also required to grant a certain proportion of their work contracts to minority businesses. In effect, the push was to integrate not only the workplace but also the boardroom. The administration of President Richard Nixon, which established the U.S. Small Business Association, continued the effort to nurture small and minority businesses.

Affirmative action also affected colleges and universities. They were mandated to initiate programs to increase the number of minorities on their campuses. In many cases, the goal was to establish proportional representation. In other words, the percentage of minority students should be roughly in line with the percentage in society in general. This meant trying to achieve a black representation in student bodies of about 10 percent.

Toward that end, race was taken into account in the admissions procedures of many of the top institutions across the country. At the time, minorities were woefully underrepresented. Affirmative action was an attempt to rectify that injustice. The programs significantly altered the make up of the student bodies at major universities.

THE *BAKKE* CASE

As the 1970s ended, a backlash against affirmative action developed. Things came to a head in 1978 with a U.S. Supreme Court case involving Alan Bakke. Bakke, who was white, had applied to the medical school at the University of California at Davis. He had been rejected, even though his grades and other credentials were excellent. The university had admitted 100 applicants that year. Of those, 84 won admission by competing against all other applicants, including Bakke. Meanwhile, the school had saved 16 seats for minority and disadvantaged applicants, ensuring that some of them would be admitted. Bakke's credentials were better than those of some minority applicants who won admission. Bakke would have won one seat given to a minority applicant, his legal team argued, if everyone had competed on a level playing field.

In a confusing ruling, the Supreme Court said that race could be taken into account in university admissions. But it made a distinction between including and excluding an applicant. Race could be a factor when including an applicant, but not when excluding an applicant. The university's affirmative action policy had excluded Bakke. Bakke's rights had been violated, and the Court ordered that he be admitted.

Times were changing, and many whites approved of the *Bakke* decision. They felt that the civil rights movement had gone far enough. Others found the decision confusing and self-contradictory.

A RAINBOW COALITION

By the late 1970s, most Black Panther leaders were jailed, exiled, killed, or scattered. When Ronald Reagan ran for president in 1980, he attacked affirmative action efforts as "reverse discrimination." On election day, he won a resounding victory.

As some people saw it, Reagan's eight years in office brought less enforcement of affirmative action. He cut funding to federal agencies that enforced civil rights laws. He appointed judges who were seemingly unsympathetic to those laws.

But the civil rights movement did enjoy a number of successes in those years. The NAACP gained ground in desegregating public schools in the North. Through the Opportunities Industrialization Centers of America (OICA), founder Leon Sullivan convinced American industry to hire more minorities.

And when Jesse Jackson ran for the presidency in 1984, he captured over 20 percent of the Democratic votes. "Our flag is red, white and blue," Jackson said. "But our nation is a rainbow—red, yellow, brown, black, and white. . . . America is not like a blanket—one piece of unbroken cloth, the same color, the same texture, the same size. America is more like a quilt—many patches, many pieces, many colors, many sizes, all woven and held together by a common thread." He founded a new organization, the Rainbow Coalition, to bring people of different races and religions together. It merged with PUSH in 1985.

Jackson ran for the presidency again in 1988. By then the United States had made some progress in race relations. The Democratic Party, which had refused to seat the black delegates from Mississippi in 1964, was now a party of inclusion. There were more black executives in corporate America. More black workers had jobs.

Still, the nation elected a conservative president that year. George Bush Sr. continued the trends of the Reagan years. The civil rights community bristled when legal champion Thurgood Marshall retired from the Supreme Court and Bush appointed Clarence Thomas to replace him. Although black, Thomas had long opposed affirmative action. On the other hand, Bush drew praise from civil rights champions when he named General Colin Powell to head the Joint Chiefs of Staff in 1989. Powell became the first black and the youngest man ever to occupy the U.S. military's top post. In January 2001, President George W. Bush named Powell U.S. secretary of state.

General Colin Powell in 1990. Powell later became one of the most powerful people in the United States as U.S. secretary of state.

EPILOGUE: A NEW DAY RISING

Looking back, it's easy to see that many laws passed along the way were major victories for civil rights. Most significant was the Voting Rights Act of 1965. When it was passed, about 100 African Americans had been elected to office in the United States. More than 7,200 held office by 1989.

The American civil rights movement no doubt influenced the world. "We Shall Overcome" was on the lips of South Africans during their long struggle against apartheid. Its lyrics were emblazoned on the shirts and headbands of student protesters in Tiananmen Square in Beijing, China, in 1989.

In 1992, when Bill Clinton, a native Arkansan, was elected president, the civil rights community gained another president who was sympathetic to their cause. At Clinton's first inauguration, he invited black poet Maya Angelou to read a poem she had prepared for the occasion. Her poem called on all Americans—naming them by tribe, religion, national origin, and political stance. "Lift up your eyes upon, /This day breaking for you. /Give birth again /To the dream," she said. Clinton echoed her optimism in his own address. "There is nothing wrong with America," he declared, "that cannot be cured by what is right with America."

Their hope for healing was underscored in 1993. Byron de la Beckwith was finally convicted of murdering Medgar Evers in Mississippi thirty years before. His hatred died with him in 2001.

In 1997 Arkansas honored the Little Rock Nine at a fortieth anniversary celebration. The event reunited Elizabeth Eckford, the girl who arrived alone at Central High in 1957, and Hazel Bryan Massery, the girl photographed jeering at Elizabeth from behind. Massery had apologized to Eckford in 1962. "I grew up in segregated society, and I thought that was the way it was," Massery said. "I don't want to pass [that bias] along to another generation." Eckford and Massery expressed hope that their reconciliation could be a "link between the past and the future."

Elizabeth Eckford receives an embrace from President Bill Clinton during a 1999 Congressional Gold Medal ceremony. The event honored her and other members of the Little Rock Nine for their courageous contributions in the struggle for racial equality.

By most measures, African Americans were better off when the new millennium began than when the civil rights movement began. In 2000, for example, voters in Selma, Alabama, elected their first black mayor. By 2002, John Lewis—the bold leader of the 1965 march in Selma—was serving his eighth term as a U.S. congressman. Bobby Frank Cherry, Thomas Blanton, and Robert Chambliss had all been convicted for the 1963 bombing of the Sixteenth Street Baptist Church in Birmingham.

Yet more progress is still needed in many areas. There is still an education gap, a health gap, and an economic gap. Many major cities still have segregated neighborhoods.

Some Americans charge that police brutality remains a threat to African American citizens. Some police departments have been accused of racial profiling (suspecting someone of criminal behavior based only on their race). Many police departments have adopted new rules to avoid racial profiling.

The discussion of racial profiling took on an international character after September 11, 2001, when Middle Eastern terrorists attacked the World Trade Center in New York City and the Pentagon in Washington, D.C. Many Americans became suspicious of any person of Middle Eastern descent. Other Americans drew on lessons learned from the civil rights movement as they cautioned against racial stereotyping.

"To suffer in a righteous cause is to grow to our humanity's full stature . . . ," Martin Luther King Jr. once said. "We need the vision to see the ordeals of this generation as the opportunity to transform ourselves and American society."

In the future, Americans face many challenges before becoming the colorblind society Martin Luther King Jr. hoped for. But clearly the ordeals of the civil rights movement gave Americans the opportunity to live up to the promise of the Declaration of Independence: "We hold these truths to be self evident, that all men are created equal." Together, the people of the civil rights movement showed that the United States can be what it was intended to be—a land of liberty and justice for all.

TIMELINE

1952	Malcolm X begins preaching in Boston, Massachusetts.
May 17, 1954	U.S. Supreme Court strikes down segregated schools with *Brown* decision.
December 1, 1955	Rosa Parks arrested; Montgomery, Alabama, bus boycott follows.
August 28, 1955	Emmett Till kidnapped and murdered in Mississippi.
February 1956	University of Alabama students riot after Autherine Lucy enrolls.
November 13, 1956	U.S. Supreme Court rules against segregation on buses.
September 9, 1957	Civil Rights Act of 1957 passed.
September 23, 1957	Little Rock Nine begin school at Central High in Little Rock, Arkansas.
February 1, 1960	Greensboro Four stage sit-ins in Greensboro, North Carolina.
November 8, 1960	John F. Kennedy elected president.
May 4, 1961	Freedom Riders depart Washington, D.C.
September 22, 1961	Interstate Commerce Commission reinforces laws against segregation in transportation facilities.
November 1961	Voter registration drive in Albany, Georgia.
April 1962	CORE, SNCC, NAACP, SCLC, and the National Urban League collaborate in voter education efforts.
April 12, 1963	Martin Luther King Jr. arrested in Birmingham, Alabama.
May 6–10, 1963	Birmingham police turn dogs and fire hoses on child marchers and clash with blacks in first urban race riots.
June 11, 1963	Alabama governor George Wallace blocks entry to University of Alabama to keep blacks out.
August 28, 1963	March on Washington in Washington, D.C.
September 1963	Four-year-old Sonnie Hereford becomes first child to integrate Alabama schools.

September 15, 1963	Bombing of Sixteenth Street Baptist Church kills four girls in Birmingham.
June 11, 1963	Medgar Evers assassinated in Mississippi.
November 22, 1963	President John F. Kennedy assassinated in Texas; Lyndon Johnson succeeds him.
July 2, 1964	Lyndon Johnson signs Civil Rights Act of 1964.
Summer 1964	Freedom Summer; six people murdered in Mississippi, including Andrew Goodman, James Chaney, and Michael Schwerner.
August 25, 1964	Mississippi Freedom Democratic Party challenges Democratic National Convention.
February 1, 1965	Seven hundred civil rights protesters jailed in Selma, Alabama.
February 25, 1965	Jim Jackson dies after being shot by state trooper in Selma.
February 21, 1965	Malcolm X assassinated in Harlem, New York.
March 7, 1965	Bloody Sunday in Selma; marchers prevented from leaving city.
March 9, 1965	Selma marchers again prevented from leaving; James Reeb dies two days later.
March 21, 1965	Lyndon Johnson sends federal troops to Selma, and marchers leave city. Viola Liuzzo murdered for driving some protesters back home to Selma.
August 6, 1965	Lyndon Johnson signs Voting Rights Act of 1965.
August 11, 1965	Six days of riots in Watts, California, begin; thirty-four people die.
June 6, 1966	James Meredith begins his March against Fear.
October 15 1966	Black Panther Party formed.
January 7, 1966	Martin Luther King Jr. launches protests in Chicago, Illinois.
1966–1967	Riots in Chicago, Cleveland, Detroit, Newark, and other cities reveal black fury at high unemployment, poverty, and police treatment.

1967	Louis Farrakhan becomes Nation of Islam national leader.
April 4, 1968	Martin Luther King Jr. assassinated in Memphis, Tennessee. Riots follow in 125 cities.
June 4, 1968	Democratic presidential candidate Robert F. Kennedy assassinated in Los Angeles, California.
1968	A national fair housing bill outlaws discrimination in housing.
1969	U.S. Supreme Court declares school segregation must end immediately.
1971	Jesse Jackson founds People United to Save Humanity (PUSH).
1978	U.S. Supreme Court rules against racial quotas in *Bakke* case.
1979	African American Richard Arrington elected mayor of Birmingham, Alabama.
1980s	George Wallace appoints African Americans to state office in Alabama.
1984	Jesse Jackson runs for president.
1985	PUSH merges with Jesse Jackson's Rainbow Coalition.
November 1986	African American John Lewis elected to U.S. Congress from congressional district in Atlanta, Georgia.
April 1992	Police beat African American Rodney King in Los Angeles, California; riots follow.
1990s	Byron de la Beckwith convicted of the murder of Medgar Evers; more convictions in civil rights murder cases follow.
2001	General Colin Powell becomes U.S. secretary of state.
2001	Bobby Frank Cherry is convicted of the 1963 bombing of the Sixteenth Street Baptist Church in Birmingham.

IN THEIR OWN WORDS

In writing this book, the author used many primary sources—documents written by living witnesses and participants in the civil rights movement. Following are two excerpts from significant primary sources of the civil rights era.

"I HAVE A DREAM"

I am happy to join with you today in what will go down in history as the greatest demonstration for freedom in the history of our nation. . . . I am not unmindful that some of you have come here out of excessive trials and tribulation. . . . You have been the veterans of creative suffering. Continue to work with the faith that unearned suffering is redemptive. . . .

Even though we must face the difficulties of today and tomorrow, I still have a dream. It is a dream deeply rooted in the American dream that one day this nation will rise up and live out the true meaning of its creed: We hold these truths to be self-evident, that all men are created equal.

I have a dream that one day on the red hills of Georgia, sons of former slaves and sons of former slave-owners will be able to sit down together at the table of brotherhood.

I have a dream that one day, even the state of Mississippi, a state sweltering with the heat of injustice, sweltering with the heat of oppression, will be transformed into an oasis of freedom and justice.

I have a dream my four little children will one day live in a nation where they will not be judged by the color of their skin but by the content of their character. I have a dream today!

I have a dream that one day every valley shall be exalted, every hill and mountain shall be made low, the rough places shall be made plain, and the crooked places shall be made straight, and the glory of the Lord will be revealed and all flesh shall see it together.

This is our hope. This is the faith that I go back to the South with.

— Dr. Martin Luther King Jr.
March on Washington, D.C., August 28, 1963

WHAT WE WANT, WHAT WE BELIEVE

1. We want freedom. We want power to determine the destiny of our Black Community.

2. We want full employment for our people.

3. We want an end to the robbery by the white man of our Black Community.

4. We want decent housing, fit for shelter of human beings.

5. We want education for our people that exposes the true nature of this decadent American society. We want education that teaches us our true history and our role in the present-day society.

6. We want all black men to be exempt from military service.

7. We want an immediate end to police brutality and murder of black people.

8. We want freedom for all black men held in federal, state, county, and city prisons and jails.

9. We want all black people when brought to trial to be tried in court by a jury of their peer group or people from their black communities, as defined by the Constitution of the United States.

10. We want land, bread, housing, education, clothing, justice, and peace. And as our major political objective [a vote] in which only black colonial subjects will be allowed to participate, for the purpose of determining the will of black people as their national destiny.

— **Black Panthers,** *party platform statement, October 1966*

SELECTED BIBLIOGRAPHY

Bennett, Lerone, Jr. *Before the Mayflower: A History of Black America.* 5th ed. New York: Penguin Books, 1984.

Branch, Taylor. *Parting the Waters: America in the King Years, 1954–63.* New York: Simon and Schuster, 1988.

Breitman, George. *The Last Year of Malcolm X: The Evolution of a Revolutionary.* New York: Schocken Books, 1967.

Canteroro, Ellen. *Moving the Mountain: Women Working for Social Change.* Old Westbury, NY: Feminist Press, 1980.

Carawan, Guy, and Candie Carawan. *We Shall Overcome! Songs of the Southern Freedom Movement.* New York: Oak Publications, 1963.

Carmichael, Stokeley, and Charles Hamilton. *Black Power: The Politics of Liberation in America.* New York: Vintage Press, 1967.

Gregory, Dick. *No More Lies.* New York: Harper & Row, 1971.

King, Martin Luther, Jr. *Why We Can't Wait.* New York: Harper & Row, 1964.

Rubel, David. *Fannie Lou Hamer: From Sharecropping to Politics.* Englewood Cliffs, NJ: Silver Burdett Press, 1990.

Sullivan, Leon. *Alternatives to Despair.* Valley Forge, PA: Judson Press, 1972.

Williams, Juan. *Eyes on the Prize: American Civil Rights Years, 1954–1965.* New York: Penguin Books, 1987.

Wright, Roberta Hughes. *The Birth of the Montgomery Bus Boycott.* Southfield, MI: Charro Press, 1991.

FURTHER READING AND WEBSITES

Darby, Jean. *Martin Luther King, Jr.* Minneapolis: Lerner Publications, 1990. This biography of Dr. King also introduces his philosophy and explains key events in the civil rights movement.

King, Casey, and Linda Barrett Osborne. *Oh Freedom! Kids Talk about the Civil Rights Movement with the People Who Made It Happen.* New York: Alfred A. Knopf, 1997. Young people, black and white, who lived during the civil rights era share their true life experiences.

Levin, Ellen. *Freedom's Children: Young Civil Rights Activists Tell Their Own Stories.* New York: G. P. Putnam's Sons, 1993. This book draws on the author's interviews with adults who grew up as civil rights activists.

Levy, Debbie. *Lyndon B. Johnson.* Minneapolis: Lerner Publications, 2003. This fine biography of President Johnson includes the story of his long-time advocacy for civil rights.

Lucas, Eileen. *Cracking the Wall: The Struggles of the Little Rock Nine.* Minneapolis: Carolrhoda Books, 1997. The students of the Little Rock Nine had grown up when they talked with the author and shared their memories of Central High.

Parks, Rosa, and Gregory J. Reed. *Dear Mrs. Parks: A Dialogue with Today's Youth.* New York: Lee & Low Books, 1996. Mrs. Parks shares her life story in this fine book.

<http://www-dept.usm.edu/~mcrohb/> The *Civil Rights Documentation Project* site offers oral history audio clips and transcripts, as well as a civil rights timeline.

<http://www.unc.edu/depts/sohp/SOHPweb/Freedomsongs.htm> *A Force More Powerful: Nashville, 1960—Freedom Songs* features clips of three freedom songs of the civil rights movement.

INDEX

ABOUT THE AUTHOR

Reggie Finlayson holds a master's degree in journalism from Marquette University in Milwaukee, Wisconsin, and teaches at the Milwaukee Area Technical College. He has written many plays and is the author of several books for young readers that seek to preserve the history of African and African-American people, including his books *Colin Powell* and *Nelson Mandela*.

ACKNOWLEDGMENTS

Photographs and illustrations used with permission of: National Archives, pp. 6 [NWDNS-306-SSM-4D(70)5], 9 [NWDNS-306-NT-650-4], 58 [NWDNS-306-SSM-4C(19)3]; © Archive Photos, pp. 2–3, 56; The *Tennessean*, p. 8; Schomburg Center for Research in Black Culture, pp. 12, 16, 36, 75; © Bettmann/Corbis, pp. 13, 19, 20, 23, 24, 26, 33, 40, 51, 52, 65, 68, 69; AP/Wide World Photos, pp. 15, 29, 31, 34, 48, 50, 72, 73; MPI/ Archive Photos, pp. 39, 41, 63, 64; AP/Wide World Photos/*Greensboro News and Record*, Jack Moebes, p. 43; Library of Congress (LC-USZ62-125806), p. 45; Laura Westlund, p. 46; © Flip Schulke/Corbis, p. 55; © Corbis, p. 61; Lyndon B. Johnson Library (276-10-64), p. 66; © Express/Archive Photos, p. 71 (left); © Keystone/Archive Photos, p. 71 (right); © Washington Post: reprinted by permission of the D.C. Public Library, p. 77; © UPI/Corbis, p. 78; © Roz Payne/Archive Photos, p. 79; © Leif Skoogfors/Corbis, p. 83; © AFP/Corbis, p. 85.

Front cover: National Archives [NWDNS-306-SSM-4C(35)6]
Back cover: Archive Photos

"I Have a Dream" excerpt p. 90 © copyright the Estate of Martin Luther King Jr. Reprinted by permission.

LERNER'S AWARD-WINNING PEOPLE'S HISTORY SERIES:

Accept No Substitutes! The History of American Advertising

Buffalo Gals: Women of the Old West

Don't Whistle in School: The History of America's Public Schools

Dressed for the Occasion: What Americans Wore 1620–1970

Failure Is Impossible! The History of American Women's Rights

Just What the Doctor Ordered: The History of American Medicine

Stop This War! American Protest of the Conflict in Vietnam

Thar She Blows: American Whaling in the Nineteenth Century

What's Cooking? The History of American Food

For more information, please call 1-800-328-4929 or visit www.lernerbooks.com